RIGORISM

The Influence of Willpower Upon History

LENNART SVENSSON

978-0-6452126-4-8

Rigorism:

The Influence of Willpower Upon History

Lennart Svensson

Thema Classification: NHD (European History), NHF (Asian History), QDX (Popular Philosophy).

MANTICORE PRESS
WWW.MANTICORE.PRESS

CONTENTS

INTRODUCTION

The title of this book is *Rigorism — The Influence of Willpower Upon History*. Now, you may find rigorism in a dictionary, saying that it denotes "rigidity in principle or practice." We haven't started from that point when using the concept; instead, we looked at the specific Latin word *rigor*, which means *hardness* and *military discipline*. And in this book, we use rigorism as a concept covering military rule throughout history. This theory covers instances of willpower in history, such as acting willfully in a crisis and demonstrating *responsibility with authority*, as Heinlein characterized military power.

Specifically, we use rigorism as a label for a political-historical phenomenon in a realm defined by catchwords like "the sword is mightier than the pen," "lawful military might," and "power is held by the man who controls *die Ausnahmezustand*." This use of rigorism as a term, including the example of *Ausnahmezustand*, is covered in the first chapter.

There are other definitions of rigorism. For example, the student of philosophy might refer to rigorism as "the moral system according to which, in every doubt of conscience as to the morality of a particular course of conduct, the opinion for law must be followed." In a similar, text-oriented vein, rigorism might mean "strict adherence to a principle in action, conduct, and thought, excluding any compromise or consideration of principles differing from the ground principle."

But this is not how rigorism is used in this book. Instead, we define rigorism as a new way of looking at history. The first chapter explains our interpretation of rigorism in greater detail. This will serve to differentiate it from other, more common explanations.

Our unique view of rigorism allows us to examine some of the gray areas in history. Today, almost no one focuses his studies of the past on *the influence of willpower upon history.* However, all historical actors have to sum up their will at times of crisis. As one crucial part of their role, all executive rulers are military rulers. To defend the realm, you always need an iron rod.

That is the background to this study and why we have written it. We cover the influence of willpower upon history and, more recently, in the west and the east. Beyond the "rigorously" themed chapters, there are historical topics, such as cycles of war, musical rulers, and the role of temples.

We use the concept of rigorism differently from students of philosophy, canon law, etc. However, it still covers a lot of familiar conceptual ground, using *rigorism* to obtain a different perspective on history — a willpower-driven view. The title chapter examines regimes in Sparta, Macedonia, the *Diadochi,* the late Republic, and Imperial Rome. This is followed by studies of Faustian Era figures like Napoleon, Boulanger, and de Gaulle. One pivotal focal point is Machiavelli's treatise *The Prince* and the strikingly similar text, Kauṭilya's *Arthaśāstra.*

This is not an academic paper nor an exhaustive study. We have only delineated the subject of military rule and its kaleidoscopic utterances through the ages. Hopefully, it will give the reader some fresh angles and new insights.

Härnösand, January 2022

LENNART SVENSSON

I. RIGORISM: THE INFLUENCE OF WILLPOWER UPON HISTORY

In the run-up to the Battle of Gaugamela, Darius sent Alexander a peace proposal. Alexander told his companions of the offer. His trusted aide, Parmenio, said:

> "I would accept those terms if I were Alexander."
> "So would I, by Zeus," retorted Alexander, "if I were Parmenio!"[1]

This, of course, meant that Alexander was sure of victory in the upcoming, decisive battle. And that, conversely, accepting this peace proposal would have been a half-measure. In the broader context, this is what we mean by "the influence of willpower upon history." Driven men like Alexander symbolize this willpower.

Willpower drives history. This approach will touch upon what we call "rigorism," *the military mindset:* to rule with the sword and not the pen, with coercion and command, not discussion and rhetorical persuasion. In this historical study, we will look at the syndrome of "authority with responsibility" of (predominantly) lawful military might and its kaleidoscopic transformations through the ages. The occurrence in politics of the warrior mindset, of *memento mori*, of loyally serving a great ruler in and out of battle is, historically,

---

[1] Plutarch, *The Age of Alexander*, p. 285-286.

sometimes opposed to the *clerical* mindset, symbolized in the afterthought of the adviser.

The focus in this book will be on heroes in the field, not on scribbling monks and intellectuals. However, the glorified *man on horseback* usually needs clerics. "You have conquered your empire on horseback, but you can't rule it from the horseback," as one such cleric said to a warrior. And "the pen is mightier than the sword"... agreed. However, the synthesis of the two can be rather powerful: merging a man-of-letters with a soldier, as, for example, the figures of Moltke and Clausewitz show us.

*****

Military might, the warrior mindset in politics throughout the ages, is examined. However, this is not an academic paper or a doctoral thesis. Instead, it's a pioneering study on the influence of willpower upon history.

As such, ancient Greece is a lucrative era for studying military rule. In Ancient Greece, we first find the occurrence of *tyrants*, a condottiere-style military ruler marking the transition from the Archaic period to the Classical period. This phenomenon will be discussed in Chapter Four. First, however, we will look at the two most famous Greek city-states, Athens and Sparta, and see how they wielded military might.

Athens was a democracy with a specific popular emphasis, with leaders having to resort to rhetoric and persuasion to have their way. For its part, Sparta was a more aristocratic state, with its whole society focused on preparing the men for war and women to become mothers of future warriors. It was an early example of rigorism, and it had its charm as such. And most tellingly, many prominent Athenians adored it, like Plato, Xenophon, Phocion, Cimon, and Aristides.

If we examine Sparta more closely, its rigorous traits become apparent.[2] For instance, Sparta had no protective wall; *its army was the wall.* This is conceptually attractive. No war is ever won by staying inside walls. However, today no physical traces of Sparta remain. Athens has archaeological ruins, but Sparta is gone, leaving just a memory of rigorism *à la grecque.* Athens is a symbol of *life* in all its variety, while Sparta, as a symbol, can come through as a bit sterile. This is something we have to remember when looking at rigorism throughout history. We won't denigrate this mindset.

On the contrary, we will quietly laud it — but — we should remember that rigorism isn't all there is to history. It shouldn't be taken too far. There is more to life than fighting and dying. "Fighting is easy, living is hard..."

Sparta is a linchpin in a study of rigorism for the Western World. And for this, you could start at the end, such as 190 BCE. By then, Sparta was just a shadow of its former glory. And, on top of everything, the Romans arrived and attacked their homeland — which was previously unheard of. Hitherto, Spartans had always been on expeditions attacking others.

In the 190 BCE campaign, Titus Quinctius' troops entered the city when the houses on the outskirts were set on fire. Thus, the legionaries about to enter the city had to retreat, and those already in town did the same so as not to be cut off. As a result, Quinctius ordered a general retreat and started a siege that soon resulted in surrender.

This was the end of Sparta. It became a city among others in the Roman Empire. Still, it was a final chapter worthy of this warrior state — for the city fell with tactics of attrition, it wasn't taken by storm, the enemy had tangibly entered the city space but was driven out. Thus, the Spartans could say that they were never defeated. This is recorded in Book XXXIV of *Ab Urbe Condita.*

Sparta was the prominent warrior state of Greece. During classical times it never took orders from anyone. Instead, Sparta

---

[2]   Furuhagen.

occupied a leadership role in every war it participated in; that was the unwritten rule. Hence Spartans had supreme command over both land and naval forces during the Persian War. The latter part is a bit odd since Sparta was no maritime power. This was predominantly Athen's domain. However, Themistocles swallowed his pride and let the Spartan Eurybiades become the navy commander to secure Sparta's war participation. Eurybiades was the leader de facto with Themistocles, the superficial naval tactician, as a chief of staff. That way, the Battle of Salamis was won.

Spartans were the greatest warriors of Greece. And a Spartan, having received an order, was bound to fulfill it, dead or alive. This can explain the defeat at Thermopylae, where the Spartans were only a small detachment facing the whole, tens-of-thousand strong Persian army. The Hellenic war council had decided that the pass must be held, and the Spartan commander on the scene, Leonidas, told the other states' contingents that they could retreat if they wanted to, the struggle would be hopeless — but they themselves, the Spartans, would at least stay. And this they did, being eventually defeated, overpowered, and killed in action. Therefore the epigram, hewn into the rock at this place:

> O xein ', aggéllein Lakedaimoníois, hóti têde
> keímetha, tois keínôn hrêmasi peithómenoi.
> Go tell the Spartans, thou who passest by,
> that here obedient to their laws we lie.

This faithfulness to orders also had another side. The following year, when fighting the Persians at Plataea, a Spartan force had been ordered to hold a particular place, but then it was re-grouped for sound reasons. However, the Spartan sub-commander in question refused; there he had been placed, there he would stay...! Soon, however, he agreed, the redistribution was completed, and the Hellenes won the ensuing battle, the final battle of the war.

Due to their leadership role, the Spartans didn't follow Alexander's Asian campaign. If they did, they would be forced to serve under Macedonians. This is the background to Alexander's following inscription concerning spoils from the Battle of Granicus: "Alexander, son of Philip, and all Greeks except for the Spartans, won these spoils from the barbarians living in Asia."

But the Spartans were not mad at Alexander because of this war. Plutarch explains how a Spartan later visited Alexander in Persia; they went on a hunt where the king came to fight with a lion. The Spartan then said, "Alexander, you fought vigorously with this lion to decide who was king!"

Sparta had kings of its own, two actually, a system called a *diarchy*. Sparta was also well-known for its unequal constitution, only giving native Spartans the right to vote, and there were not many. Then there were foreign residents (*perioikoi*) with a half-favored status and large numbers of slaves or *Helots*, the original indigenous people of Lacedaemon. They were defeated when the Spartans/Dorians invaded the region. The degree of oppression is illustrated by the fact that an essential task of a Spartan army on the march is said to have been watching the weapons when camped to prevent the food-cooking and serving Helots from grabbing the arms and rebelling. For instance, when Sparta suffered from an earthquake in 464 BCE, there was indeed an attempt at a Helot insurgency, but because King Archidamus called the Spartans to arms before the invasion, this revolt was nipped in the bud.

The Spartans ate rough bread, black porridge, and exercised daily. Their main goal in life was war and breeding new warriors for the state. This could give you the impression that the state was nothing more than a military camp in a sterile environment, disregarding culture and cultivation. Indeed, it was much more of a warrior state than other Greek states, but there were also redeeming features. For example, the landscape where Sparta was situated, the plain of Eurotas, was particularly fertile, drained by four rivers which then flowed into the Eurotas, which mouthed in the bay of Laconia.

The Spartans practiced choral singing, mainly of a nationalist kind regarding culture. However, there were also the Spartan women, famed for their beauty. A 12 cm high bronze figure illustrates this, depicting a fresh, sporty, and charming Spartan girl dressed in a skirt with a waist belt doing justice to her body.

Spartan women had considerably great sexual freedom, according to the author Károly Kerényi. Regarding sexuality, homosexuality was — in a way — encouraged among the Spartan men who lived in shared dorms from seven years of age to their middle age. But the Spartans were not women haters; textual sources speak of how much the Spartans loved their women.

*****

The Spartans obeyed their laws. And so did the Athenians. However, in the Athenian culture, the people's courts lacked juridical competence, and bribes and political concerns ruled the system. Also, as soon as any Athenian achieved some greatness (Themistocles, Cimon, Aristides, etc.), he was expelled: the institute of ostracism.

Sparta was heroic; Athens became a babbling quagmire. That's the standard view, but it isn't that simple. One Athenian who was a reliable commander in the field and had mastered the style of debate and persuasion was Phocion. He was a fine example of balanced rigorism, of will-and-thought combined. His enemy was Demosthenes, a lawyer that was opposed to Macedonian expansion. Concerning Demosthenes, it was said that:

> *Eíper ísên rômên gnômê, Dêmósthenes, eiches,*
> *Oúpot' àn hellênon êrxen Árês Makedôn.*
> If only your strength had been equal, Demosthenes, to your wisdom,
> never would Greece have been ruled by a Macedonian Ares.

Demosthenes tried to withstand the Macedonian expansion into Greece proper. And for this, he has been hailed as a hero. However, according to Plutarch, he was subsided by Persian gold, which at the time was prolific. Demosthenes couldn't resist the allure of gold. So, latter-day historians who dislike generals and admire clerics should look elsewhere for an idol. Demosthenes possessed too much thought (*gnômê*) and too little will (*rômê*).

Phocion, his opponent, was more adaptive towards the Macedonian challenge; maybe not as heroic, but he was a realist. And, for Athens, he was a rigorist paragon. One anecdote pits the two against each other, the general and the speaker. Demosthenes once said:

> One of these days, Phocion, the Athenians will kill you, if they lose their heads," to which Phocion replied, "Yes, but they will kill you, if they get them back again.[3]

There are more anecdotes highlighting the wit of Phocion, a down-to-earth, *"res, non verba"* speaking style, against which Demosthenes's formal rhetoric, composed first in writing and then recited in public, falls flat. "Demosthenes was the best orator, but Phocion was the most effective speaker."[4] Phocion was a Moltke of his time who focused on keeping his speeches short. For example, Phocion was once seen ruminating before a speech. A friend, asking what was on his mind, got this answer from Phocion: "I am thinking out whether I can shorten the speech I am going to make to the Athenians."[5]

This is reminiscent of Moltke's succinct manner of expression — in orders and social circumstances. Therefore, I hereby give the floor to Alexander Kluge and his *Schlachtbeschreibung*:

> There was a bet before the Emperor's birthday that Moltke the Elder's toast to the Emperor would be of less than ten

---

[3]   Plutarch, *The Age of Alexander*, p. 226.

[4]   Ibid, p. 222.

[5]   Ibid.

words, address and the first hurrah included. Moltke said: Gentlemen, long live the Emperor![6]

During the war against the Macedonian king Antipater (the so-called Lamian War), Phocion advised the Athenians not to go to war. But, someone retorted, would the time never come when Phocion would advise Athens to actually make war? Phocion replied:

> Yes, She can go to war when I see the young men willing to observe discipline, the rich to make contributions, and the demagogues to refrain from embezzling public funds.[7]

This is a striking picture of Athens during its time of decline, a state despised by Phocion. He expected nothing from it. Once, after having received a warm applause in the parliament for something he said, he remarked to his friends: "Can it be that I have been arguing on the wrong side without knowing it?"[8] This is similar to Oscar Wilde's saying: "When people agree with me, I always feel I must be wrong..."

*****

In one of the battles of the Lamian War, Phocion had distributed the Athenian army in battle order, with the enemy facing them. Then one of his soldiers ran out from the ranks to the center of the field, and at the same time, a soldier came out from the enemy's ranks to meet him. The stage was set for a pre-battle duel, that old *"pars pro toto"* ritual. However, when seeing the other man, the Athenian became scared and ran back. Phocion said, "Young man, you ought to be ashamed at deserting your post twice in one day, first the position which I gave you, and then the one you gave yourself."[9]

---

[6] Kluge, p. 265; my translation.

[7] Plutarch, *The Age of Alexander*, p. 237.

[8] Ibid, p. 225.

[9] Ibid, p. 239.

Phocion was killed on orders from the Athenian rulers at the decree of the ruler of Macedonia. The accusation was made in the context that Phocion had assisted Macedonia during the time of Alexander, betraying his land, but that Athens now would regain its old freedom; what a casuistry. However, when Phocion was to be executed, they were out of poison because he was the last in line to be executed. And the poison mixer refused to prepare more poison unless he was paid. But Phocion arranged payment via a friend and could eventually empty the cup of poison hemlock. So you could say that he magnanimously paid for the rope he was hanged with.

*****

The Macedonian era was a field day for the rigorist. Finally, we obtain a monarch and can depart from the previous Hellenic craze of quarrels and legal hairsplitting behind. Even Sparta had two "kings" to lead them in a diarchy like the Roman consulship but unsatisfactory for ruling an empire. Promoting loyalty to the king (singular), fighting and death in the field of honor, and a society of aristocratic warriors — this was the new style of rigorism that arose when Alexander stepped onto the stage of history.

We will elaborate further on Alexander in chapter four. First, however, here we must mention this one anecdote explaining Alexander's character *in nuce,* from the night before the Battle of Gaugamela, which would be the final, decisive blow against the Persian Empire. On the plain in question, Alexander saw the campfires of the Persians spread out before him, indicating the enemy army was nearby. "Shouldn't we attack at once?" someone asked, but Alexander replied:

I will not steal my victory.

A noble answer. And Alexander was genuinely great, "the stuff that legends are made of." Every Eurasian culture has a legend concerning Alexander. As for the era he founded, it can be added that he was

15

a cut above the rest, especially his successors. The only thing the *Diadochi* had in common was infamy, Demetrius the Besieger being a case in point. One subject in his realm, an old woman, once sought him out for advice. But he just said that he didn't have time for this. "Then don't be king!" the woman said. A resounding reply from the masses, reminding every ruler to take responsibility for what he is, brought to us by Plutarch.[10]

From the perspective of government, state-building, and long-term political formations, the Alexandrian Empire surmounted to naught — like all Greek *Realpolitik* endeavors, one is tempted to add. The Delian League, the Spartan hegemony, the Theban Sacred Band were also short-lived — and, in harmony with this "fine" tradition, Alexander's empire simply fell apart after its triumph. It became just another mid-eastern governance, having nothing of the Roman state-building strain to it. However, it has to be admitted that the Byzantine Empire, the last Greek political creation of antiquity, lasted for almost a thousand years. Due, perhaps, to its adherence to glorious rigorism, a strict military rule shunning debate and bickering.

*****

Rome's first overseas venture was to fight the city-state of Carthage. We won't go into detail but merely mention a fascinating, esoteric side note. According to spiritualist writer David Wilcock Hannibal, the star of the Second Punic War, invaded the Italian mainland, won a great tactical victory at Cannae, and after finally being beaten at Zama in North Africa, was later reincarnated as Adolf Hitler...![11]

---

[10]   (Life of Demetrius in *The Age of Alexander*).

[11]   Details aside, it makes sense, the two men having this in common: being willful warrior types, their careers seeing success in the early parts of them followed by setbacks in the later parts, and their attitude of "taking on the whole world, not yielding to superior force." Also, when looking at the Hannibal marble bust found in Capua, you can note some odd similarities to Hitler. That they started their wars 2,160 years apart, an astrological age, is also seen as being of some

****

We now turn to the Mediterranean War of 168-133 BCE. In the Rome of this era, we find a republic with a fetish for law and procedure, such as having the two consuls alternating their command of the army each day. Equality, yes, sound military leadership, no. The Cannae campaign is a case in point; it was Rome's most decisive tactical defeat. *One* commander is the way to conduct a war; his is the glory, his is the blame. Responsibility comes with authority. Rome knew the advantages of this too, in the form of the dictatorship institution, bestowing all the state's power into one hand. But *dictator* was a temporary tenure, to be used in emergencies, and Sulla's and Caesar's tendency to make themselves permanent dictators wasn't well received. They seemed on the way to becoming kings, a taboo for the Roman republicans, having founded their state by overthrowing a monarchy. However, with time, with its monarchic taboo overridden, Rome becomes a splendid, rigorous monarchy and a lasting one. We will revisit the Roman concept of kingship in chapter four.

*****

The Romans knew the art of empire. They knew how to build one that would last. You could say it was done by adhering to high principles, like having a devout religious attitude towards deals entered with other nations. *"Fiat Justitia, et pereat mundus"* — freely translated, "dead or alive, justice must be done." A deal was an oath sworn before the gods, hence the "medieval" faithfulness to them.

In this way, the Italian peninsula was conquered. It's been said that the emerging Roman rule was more of a "hegemony system" than a rule built on dominance on submission. Rome didn't want to extend its own sovereignty; it only wanted to abolish others.

---

importance: like, subtracting 2,160 from 1939 you get 221 BCE, the year Hannibal became Carthaginian C-i-C. The place to check out this theory is Wilcock's *The Synchronicity Key* (2013).

In the 100s BCE, however, Rome developed a more imperialistic approach. Fraud and lies, deportation, and plunder became the order of the day. For instance, take the Macedonian War. Rome went to war with Macedonia on dubious grounds, ceased it, and sliced it into four provinces. Its officials were deported, the gold mines were ransacked, and its king Perseus was brought along in chains in the triumph of Aemilius Paulus.

In the context of this war, Corinth was ravaged in 146 BCE as a punishment for an assault on Roman diplomats; the citizens were sold as slaves, and the city's lavish art treasures were sent to Rome. Plunder was by then the order of the day in Roman warfare.

Further proof of Roman severity came in the Third Punic War. In the final stage, the war zone had virtually engulfed the entire city of Carthage itself. Finally, however, the Carthaginians agreed to hear a proposal for a settlement after laying down their arms. Once this was done, they were told that the plan was to leave their city and move inland. This resulted in a desperate battle, but Rome won and razed Carthage to the ground. This happened in the middle of the 100s BCE.

Hard measures and cunning were the order of the day then. For example, according to Bjöl & Hjortsö, Spain had a case where the Romans had been plundering for about 200 years. As a consequence of some rebellions, the Roman measures resulted in massacres and deportations. In 180 BCE, the situation became a bit more tranquil, but in 154, another rebellion broke out. Servius Sulpicius Galba had promised some of the rebellious tribes that they would be given land if they laid down their weapons, but instead, he simply killed them or sold them as slaves. The money he gained there was used in Rome for bribery so that he remained free from punishment. Earlier, the Romans had established themselves as a master race in Spain. Contractual reciprocity was seldom found in the relationship, with the Spaniards being told to acknowledge the *imperium et majestas* of Rome, its domination and supremacy. The Romans exhibited a mighty arrogance, systematic conquest, and plunder during these years. Livy called the phenomenon *nova sapientia*, "the new cunning" (Book XLII).

However, as intimated, it hadn't always been this way. In the olden times, the Romans were known for their adherence to *fides*: faithfulness, reliability, and conscientiousness. This was the fundament of Roman empire-building. Rome acted as *a patron of its clients*, like a local strongman does, in a feudal manner protecting his underlings in return for diverse favors. A sworn oath was overseen by the gods and had to be fulfilled, no matter what. That was the mentality of the early Republic, such as during the Italic Wars of the 300s BCE when Rome was eager to fulfill its obligations for allies. For example, when Rome's ally Luceria asked for help, Rome listened and came to the rescue, despite Rome itself not being threatened.

Furthermore, in this campaign, Rome suffered a crushing defeat against the Samaritans in the Caudine Passes. It did not matter — because compliance with an alliance commitment was the order of the day in the prevailing Roman style in politics. It was about securing Rome's credibility as an alliance partner.

A focus on principles, not on petty material goals, was the watchword. This aspect didn't vanish entirely in the late republican era. For example, Caesar in the Gallic Wars rescued the Boioi so that Rome wouldn't face the shame of having left an ally in the lurch, thereby losing the sympathy of all its allies.[12]

Along with the traditional, down-to-earth *Realpolitik*, there are more examples of adherence to *fides* in this war. Details aside, there was a Roman ambition to make every war into a *bellum justum*, a righteous war, and a successful way to do that was to characterize the whole enterprise as a fulfillment of an obligation. That is how Rome made war, from the Italian peninsula through Sicily, Spain, Carthage, and all the Mediterranean, to Gallia and Britain, until it was master of them all. Of course, this adherence to principles could degenerate into casuistry, a cover-up for naked conquest. However, the Roman reputation was primarily built on its credibility as an

---

12 *The Gallic War*, Book Seven.

alliance partner, which, in turn, rested on the religious belief in respecting sworn oaths.

In an overall strategic sense, Roman republican warfare was based on a central political power, whereby the senate in Rome made decisions concerning war and peace, not the commanders in the field. This was *military might under law.* With the late Republic, when the conquests generated more conflicts, and generals and their veteran followings became a force in politics, this principle came to an end. As victorious generals, Sulla, Pompey, and Caesar became rulers in their own right. Bribes, money, and gold drove the formal-legal process of being elected consul, proconsul, etc. — gold sometimes stolen by these generals in previous campaigns. However, by being commanders (and not clerics), they staked their credibility in the process. If you didn't return to Rome with a victory under your belt, you were finished as a leader. This was an example of responsibility as an integral part of military might.

It was no game. Crassus, essentially a money-lender and banker, thought it would be easy to be elected consul and lead an army against the Persians. But he was defeated (Carrhae, 59 BCE), and his severed head was thrown before the Sassanid ruler as a final token of humiliation. So you had to know your way as a commander. Pompey was virtually born in a field camp. According to Fuller [1965], Caesar didn't start studying military matters until he was in his forties, but when he put his mind to it, Caesar excelled in the art of war.

*****

Regarding warriors and clerics, we intimated this earlier when describing the conflict concerning "Demosthenes vs. Phocion" and in the anecdote at the beginning, where Alexander is the warrior, and Parmenio plays the clerical role. Willpower versus (after)thought, tangible drive versus deliberation, the pen versus the sword. All this, however, reveals a much wider conflict, *the social conflict of warriors versus priests.*

For example, in olden times, the priest class ruled Egypt, Mesopotamia (and India before the *Mahābhārata* war, to express it in mythological terms). Then, according to Schuré, with the rise of Assyria, the warrior class came to rule Mesopotamia. At the same time, Egypt formally continued as a theocracy — although it, too, under Rameses II, had a rather formidable war machine.

In the late Roman Republic, the figure of Cicero is the symbol for this cleric-versus-warrior aspect. To pave the way for Cicero, we could also say that Rome was going through political turmoil after all the conquests of the Mediterranean War. The rise of mercenary generals, having to provide for their ranks of veterans, was one such destabilizing factor. The situation cried out for a strong leader to take charge. Marius and Sulla pioneered the style; Caesar, Crassus, and Pompey continued the syndrome. The second triumvirate from which Octavian, the future Emperor Augustus rose, completed the development, seeing Augustus as a monarch ruling the Empire. However, republican forms remained to cover up the transition.

The sword ruled during this era but a confident man of letters was present and very active during all this: Marcus Tullius Cicero. It was a precarious balance, then, against the bluntness of the mercenary generals, who surely could be brutal. A case in point is Pompey's treatment of Quintus Valerius:

> Pompey ... behaved very inhumanly in the case of Quintus Valerius. This was in a Sicilian campaign. Pompey knew that Valerius was a remarkably learned and scholarly man and, when he was brought before him, Pompey took him aside, walked up and down with him, and, after he had asked him questions and found out what he wanted to know, ordered his servants to take the man away and put him to death at once.[13]

---

[13]   Plutarch, *Fall of the Roman Republic*, p. 166-167.

21

In contrast, Cicero was a gifted writer and lawyer, winning his position with judicial rhetoric. However, sometimes his eloquence got the better of him. He lacked the imagination to realize that this "era of rigorism" was no time for irony and snide remarks, which was typical of the (inferior) intellectual. But he still used them, even in the field once. It was in the army of Pompey before Pharsalus. For example, a man just having received a command was told that he was a pleasant and sound fellow. "Why, then," said Cicero, "don't you give him a job as a schoolmaster?"[14] And Cicero said, after the defeat at Pharsalus when someone noted that there is still hope because they still had seven eagles (silver eagle is the legion's banner): "Excellent advice, if only we were fighting against jackdaws."[15]

Given the circumstances, this was needless wit. Cicero wasn't acting as would befit a Responsible Man...! He could have shaped up, for he was definitely not a clown. He was a politician and a man of the state. He should have learned from Talleyrand, another intellectual with no feeling for the rigorist lifestyle; however, he had the grace to withhold any pithy remarks when he was forced to come along on one of Napoleon's field operations, the campaign of 1805-1806.

*****

Rome lasted — at least during the Pax Romana. Peace prevailed during the first phase of imperial rule. Then, a fatal flaw became apparent. Because Rome could not conquer all the German tribes (all of the then "Germany"), Rome could not push the limes east to the Elbe, whereby the Empire, with time, became impossible to defend. Too many barbarian tribes exerted pressure on the western part of the Empire. The Eastern/Middle Eastern border lacked natural support. And then came the "soldier Emperors," as a symptom of all this; military matters became predominant in the imperial rule.

---

[14]   Plutarch, *Fall of the Roman Republic,* p. 349.

[15]   Ibid, p. 350.

However, the Romans did their utmost to create and defend their realm; they did nothing wrong politically. They just ran out of steam after a while. The new power center would lie in northern Europe, beyond the limes of the Roman empire.

*****

Speaking of intellectuals and rigorism, we must leap forward in time to Niccolò Machiavelli, a central figure in this respect. He has even been put forth as a warning: "the father of fascism!" He did indeed teach the monarch how to rule with an iron hand, but that isn't the whole picture. Rigorism, monarchy, and the rule of the sword weren't all he knew, although this is the subject of *The Prince*. He also deliberated on the problems and possibilities of republican governance and political freedom in *The Discorses,* an essay based on the first ten books by Livy, which handled the Roman Republic.

According to chapter twelve of *The Prince,* Machiavelli's ideal was "good laws and good arms."[16] Again, an example of *military might under law.*

In general, *The Prince* may be a harsh doctrine. To build a lasting state, Machiavelli advocates that you must do as the Romans did. Rule with an iron rod, strike down rebellions, deport subjugated peoples, etc. However, at least from a historical point of view, this is true. The Romans were ready to use harsh measures when incorporating new lands into their realm: Spain, Gaul, and Greece. Eventually, after a period of insecurity and insurrection, the regions became pacified. As we said above: the Greeks couldn't lastingly build empires, but the Romans could. In his study, Machiavelli sees the same pattern.

In *The Prince,* Machiavelli says many clever things. We won't go into all of them. However, this is a political rule of thumb of eternal value: if a ruler must "deal a harsh blow," he should amass and effect many such hard measures at once. On the other hand, "handing

---

[16] Machiavelli, p. 77.

out the goodies" should be done over an extended period of time. This could also make you think of the use of *negative and positive sanctions,* which we will return to in chapter eleven, *Rigorism in the East II.*

*****

Then, what to say of rigorism in the Middle Ages and the New Era? We can begin by looking at the most basic "tools of the trade," arms and armor. Simply put, during antiquity, *the infantry* ruled; from 700 BCE and long into the Current Era, the footman ruled the battlefield, in Macedonian and Carthaginian times somewhat aided by cavalry not using stirrups. Now, in medieval times, the *armored cavalryman* enters the stage. With the invention of the stirrup (originally a Chinese invention of the Tang era, 600-900 CE), a rider could get a smoother ride. The stirrups allowed him to half-stand in them without having to shake along with all the horse's movement. And, tactically, the stirrup made fighting on horseback easier. For, now the rider was supported with (1) his feet in the stirrups and (2) the left hand holding the pommel, a concept enabling you to cut and thrust with sword or spear without the risk of falling out of the saddle (as was the case previously when stirrups weren't around and every thrust you made threatened to make you fall off the horse).

This gave rise to chivalry, to the mounted knight as the decisive weapon during the high Middle Ages, a concept spilling over into the realm of politics with *feudalism.* However, social feudalism survived the rise of the infantryman in the 14th century and beyond.

Even if only symbolically, the mounted knight must be noted for shaping this era. Cavalry blossomed until the mid-19th century, with cuirassiers (heavy cavalry, the inheritor of the medieval knight), hussars (light cavalry), and dragoons (mounted infantry). The invention of firearms (cannon, musket) then came to shape the rest of the history of the art of war, with "increased firepower" as the leitmotif.

24

But the knight ruled medieval Europe, using military might with or without regulating law. A man serving the king with horse and armor received an exemption from tax, creating a system of privileges and special provisions extending until the era of revolutions, after which *equality before the law* became the standard.[17] And with "revolution" comes "republic," whereby monarchies, in the long run, only prevailed in the northern European periphery. However, in Latin European lands, this social leveling also creates a rigorist reaction, with "the man on horseback" now coming to the fore in politics. We might have seen him before, as in tyrants of Greek city-states, some *condottieri,* and the Rienzi figure in Italy.

Cromwell and the Puritans are a fine example of the man on horseback in the early modern era. They defeated the royal camp in a civil war, their case of resistance against oppression being somewhat credible — freedom of thought, the right to tax yourself. With the force of arms, the Puritans defeated the Royalists and took control of the United Kingdom, justifying their case by having God on their side. This could lead to exaggerations, but it also limited Papal persecution. For example, in the Italian Alpine region, when Protestants were harassed, Cromwell said to the Pope that if the people of God weren't treated well in Catholic lands, they would soon be hearing the thunder of English cannons in Rome. The persecution ceased.[18]

This is a splendid example of the influence of willpower upon history.

Rigorism is symbolized by "the man on horseback" in France. He has historically been a concept of some duration.

Tingsten once said (1971) that French political history had two marshals and three generals known without names. The first marshal was MacMahon, hero of Sevastopol and duke of Magenta, having

---

[17]   As such, this is a virtual repetition, a coeval/simultaneous/isochronous situation to Septimus Severus extending Roman citizenship to all free men of the Empire in 212.

[18]   Estlander, p. 132.

failed at Sedan but then going on to crush the Paris Commune to become the first president of the Third Republic. The second marshal in this respect was Pétain, rising to political prominence in the fateful year of 1940.

The first of the three generals was Napoleon in the autumn of 1799, after returning from Egypt but before the Brumaire coup. In the late 1880s, war minister Boulanger was "the general." From the 1940s and on it was de Gaulle.

As for Boulanger's career, it came to naught, but he did make some impression as a potential military ruler. His program was *Revanche, Revision, Restauration* — revenge on Germany, revision of the constitution, and a return to monarchy. One of about *400* Boulanger songs composed at the time was this:

> *Il reviendra quand le tambour battra,*
> *et l'ennemi menacera nos frontères;*
> *il reviendra, et chacun le suivra,*
> *pour cortège il aura la France entière.*

This translation is: "He will return by the beating of the drum when the enemy's threatening our borders; he will return and everyone will follow him, having all of France as his entourage."

Napoleon was a prime symbol of rigorism. Many a good anecdote can illuminate his character; for example, in 1799, when about to leave Africa and sail home, he spotted an English corvette on the horizon. Naturally, some of his company were worried. However, Napoleon just said: "Bah! We'll get there. Luck has never abandoned us. We shall get there, despite the English." He knew that he was in for greatness. Compare this to what he said at the beginning of the Russian campaign: "I feel myself impelled towards a goal with which I am unacquainted; when I shall have reached it, when I shall be no longer needed for it, an atom will suffice to throw me down, but until that moment all human efforts will be powerless against me."[19]

---

[19] Quoted after Yorck von Wartenburg.

Indeed, a Man of Destiny. Also, in the case of Napoleon, a choice quote from the run-up to the Brumaire coup was an officer saying, "If this is about throwing the lawyers into the river, count me in." This is the conflict warrior-cleric *in nuce.*

The warrior-cleric pattern is illustrated even better in the Napoleonic era, via Napoleon's relations to his secretary of state, Talleyrand. Duff Cooper, in his biography, reveals illuminating anecdotes from this former bishop, gourmet, and gambler, who, even for a cleric, was a bit aloof, such as always letting someone else write required documents. Talleyrand liked the constitutional monarchy, and during the Terror he was in exile. He was also pragmatic, so when Napoleon's rise to power began, he approached Napoleon and decided to overthrow the Directorate with him. It was a faceless, corrupt regime that followed the radical experiments by Danton and Robespierre.

With the help of Talleyrand, Napoleon, before the coup making him ruler of France, marketed himself as a modest figure. By the late 1790s, Napoleon was a noteworthy general. Still, he often donned civilian garb, and he said that he wanted to live a tranquil life dedicated to scientific study, dreaming away in the poetic realms of Ossian. Napoleon stated that he only wanted to be elected into the Institute de France, then he would retire.

Did the public believe it? Regardless, the regime was weak and easily overthrown. Talleyrand became the secretary of state; the top man was the First Consul, soon to be the Emperor — Napoleon. After successful French military campaigns, Talleyrand served him well and enriched himself while cutting up and redistributing Europe. When Talleyrand turned against him, he might have seen the end of this upstart. This began in 1807. He continued serving the Emperor, who had surmised the presence of treachery, but Napoleon couldn't prove anything. During one meeting, he insulted Talleyrand, but the prince didn't move a muscle. He only said afterward: "Such a shame that a great man should be so rude."

And, after another, similar event: "The Emperor is in a splendid mood today!"

However, all told, Talleyrand and Napoleon made a great pair in ruling Europe. The cleric well completed the style of the man on horseback. Talleyrand was no saint but his execution of *Realpolitik*, with a sense of moderation, is rather commendable.

*****

Of Spain, the following can be said of the military element in politics.[20] For instance, during the 19th-century upheavals, it was *expected* that the military should interfere. The question "Why is the military taking so long?" was asked during more than one liberal coup since the military in the 19th century did, in fact, have a liberal reputation. As late as in the 1930 coup ousting the dictator Primo de Rivera, liberal elements resorted to military means to have their way. So, we shouldn't blame the pre-1936 Spanish military for meddling in politics on its own accord. The large, primarily unoccupied Spanish officer cadre in the late 19th, early 20th century did exert a critical mass by itself, making it extend into the political realm. Post-colonial Spain had an oversized military. Defense matters aside, a small army is more conducive to a republican culture.

*****

Coup d'état generals are relatively scarce in other European realms compared to Spain and France. The 20th-century "black" and "brown" dictatorships might all be militarily influenced — but — they are run by political parties, not by scheming officer cabals. For example, Germany only ever had one (1) military dictator, which was in the form of Ludendorff during WWI. Details aside, in his rise to power, Hitler saw that this wouldn't happen again. Hitler's

---

[20]   Wretman and Olofsson.

regime wasn't a military dictatorship proper; it was the dictatorship of a political party.

Except for France and Spain (and Asia in the post-colonial era), it's Latin America that has seen explicit military rule, symbolized by "the man on horseback" as a force in politics, from Simon Bolivar and onwards. In Latin America, there were generally two kinds of military coups that prevailed: the *pronunciamento* and the *veto coup*, respectively. The former was the "visionary, idealist" coup, symbolized in the statement proclaimed by the plotters (the "pronunciamento"), announcing "down with oppression, now we will clean out the brothel and head for glory, etc." For its part, the *veto coup* was more subdued in tone, only aiming at restoring the societal situation to a perceived state of normality, the plotters saying "no" (Latin, *veto*) to the development until then.

*****

On a side note, in the high medieval era, we had epics of heroic quests, of searching for the Holy Grail, such as *Le Morte d'Arthur* and *Parsifal*. Then came the imitators, the less profound stories of heroes which were somewhat devoid of meaning and were mostly a succession of marvels upon marvels. However these late medieval so called "Amadis novels" were read, and they did make a significant impression — for instance, the Spanish conquistadores were bent on seeking similar adventures in the New World, led by "the immemorial voice of a myth."

The discovery of the New World was itself a mythical, nay, *elemental*, planet-changing event. This must be noted, despite the brutal episodes of that conquest. However, to merely say that Columbus should have stayed home and the funds for the voyage should have been spent on welfare projects in the slum of Madrid is just pure nonsense, an uttering of an anti-willpower, anti-vision, anti-everything attitude.

Willpower and vision are the driving forces of history, and Columbus embodies this.

*****

Now let's take a look at pertinent aspects of National Socialist Germany. It isn't pure rigorism. In the same vein, as we didn't support the rigorism of Sparta, we don't support that of the Third Reich either.

In a historical context, when looking at previous German regimes, you could say that National Socialist Germany played virtually the same game as they did. In propaganda, the reign of Frederick the Great was regarded as an ideal. "Don't argue; pay your taxes; report recruits that have gone AWOL" was a supposed list of civic orders in Friedrich's day. Further, implicitly, the *Second* Reich of Bismarck was an acknowledged predecessor, in that the Nazis called their state the *Third* Reich. The first Reich was the medieval Holy Roman Empire.[21]

Bismarck's Germany was rigorist. "Not through speeches and majority decisions will the great questions of the day be decided — that was the great mistake of 1848 and 1849 — but by iron and blood," Bismarck said in 1862. The painting of Wilhelm I being crowned German Emperor in the Hall of Mirrors in 1871 is a potent symbol of this, a whirl of soldiers surrounding the majesty.

The Hitler figure will always be hard to fathom. It tends to be a combination of myth and legend when dealing with *Der Führer*. Carl Jung saw the unusual character of Hitler, calling him a modern Muhammed "teaching virtue with the sword" and, when comparing Hitler to Mussolini, said that "Mussolini is a man; Hitler is a myth."[22] The mythological aspect was dwelt on at length by Miguel Serrano in *The Golden Thread* and *The Ultimate Avatar.*

---

[21]   This triad of state names was concocted by Arthur Moeller van den Bruck, 1876-1925.

[22]   Jung interviewed in *Cosmopolitan* by H. R. Knickerbocker, January 1939.

The best summation of the Hitler phenomenon was made by a general serving in the Third Reich, Walter von Brauchitsch. In Nuremberg in 1946, he said: "Hitler was the fate of Germany, and this fate could not be stayed."[23] Details aside, this kind of *amor fati* is a way to approach the Hitler complex without reducing it into a dualistic, good/bad pattern.

Earlier, we spoke of the "warrior and the cleric" in the form of Napoleon's relationship to Talleyrand. Was there a similar relationship between Hitler and Goebbels? Perhaps. But Goebbels wasn't so close to the inner circle of power. He was never a figure like Himmler or Göring. However, according to Bullock,[24] as Göring's approval waned, Goebbels's ascended. When the Reich collapsed, Goebbels joined the Führer in the Berlin bunker to meet his end.

*****

Military might has made kaleidoscopic changes through history. How do we discuss the influence of willpower upon history?

Earlier, we mentioned this trope: "authority with responsibility." This is a formula to remember when wanting to vindicate the military mindset in politics. Heinlein suggested it. Of course, there is much more to politics than being a legalistic cleric. The military man, acknowledging law, is *one* key to responsible government. And in the post-war era, former military officers like Eisenhower, Yasuhiro Nakasone, and Helmut Schmidt have done rather well as leaders of their respective lands. The prime example is Charles de Gaulle, probably the last European leader worthy of his name since 1945.

However, the state can't be run without clerics. The clerics must have a responsible, "military" mindset not to become corrupt. They require ideals of service, duty, and honor. In Japan, during the modern era, there was very little corruption due to former *samurais*

---

[23]   Bullock.

[24]   1966, p. 180.

making up the civil servant corps. Compare this to China, a land run by clerics since way back and afflicted by more corruption. The warrior has high ideals, do right and live, do wrong and die — the ethos of the battlefield. The cleric is more of a lithe figure, clouding his doings in rhetorical casuistry.

This must be remembered when speaking of the warrior versus the cleric.

*****

All rulers are military rulers. All the world's executive leaders — presidents, prime ministers, etc. — must be ready to use the force of arms. To defend the realm, military might is needed, and akin to this military power is the use of force in an everyday sense. To uphold law and order, prioritizing the institutions of police and the judiciary is a way of using force in politics. All politicians must do it; some are open about it; some are silent about it. The former are honest; the latter are cowardly, afraid to estrange themselves from flimsy voters.

In a philosophical vein, you can say that, ultimately, the executive ruler derives his might from declaring martial law. This is because he who holds sovereign power controls the *Ausnahmezustand* — the state of martial law. This is what Carl Schmitt meant, and we hope that today's saintly political leaders would acknowledge this too, seeing military might as an integral part of political power, and not just looking at the military as a tool stored under a plate of glass and a sign saying, "break in case of war"...

As Adlai Stevenson said: "Power corrupts, but lack of power corrupts absolutely." Therefore, any ruler must exert power; any governance must be built on lasting power. And wielding military might under law, the ruler is "armed and free."[25] Not that we want soldiers in the streets. That's not a way to rule a land. However, there are different ways of exerting power. There is *punishing* power ("do

---

[25]   Machiavelli, p. 79.

32

as I say, or I will punish you"). There is *rewarding* power ("do as I say, and I will reward you"). And there is *persuasive* power ("please, do as I say"). In today's debate, power is almost only seen as examples of two and three. Most seem to have forgotten that politics also, and maybe primarily, is the use of force.

II. CYCLES OF WAR

1. Total Wars and Limited Wars

I hate war, it destroys armies ...

This was said by Konstantin Pavlovich (1779-1831), a Russian grand duke and officer who fought in the Napoleonic wars. Since this was an era of total war, you can understand his lament. Total war is an elementary phenomenon, harrowing like a natural disaster. For isn't it better to have a *limited* war, more manageable with its chess-style maneuvering...? In such a war, you know what to expect.

This chapter examines European wars, noting how total wars alternate with more limited ones. It utilizes a unique idea of *cycles of war* or an outline of the morphology of war. For there is a distinction between different wars: we have those that are total and all-embracing, and we have those that are more limited in nature. In Europe, since the late 15th century, these two kinds of war alternate with a certain degree of regularity.

Today, the implicit historical model seems to be linear: it's getting better and better with time, everything "develops," everything progresses. However, without denying all forms of progress, we claim a different approach, a cyclic one. We will depict European wars from 1494 onwards, making sense of them in a structural way.

We will also capture their prevalent mood, sentiment, and mentality: what makes some wars long and bitter while others are shorter and more decent in nature.

Some wars are total. They seem to be fought in an atmosphere of "break and bend," as Clausewitz observed. Conversely, he also saw that other wars had an overall atmosphere of "observe and negotiate." That is, a mentality of limiting the actions of violence.

The ancient symbol for *total war* is the Peloponnesian War. It lasted for nearly thirty years, was fought with resentment, and had a "false peace" in the middle of it (the Peace of Nicias). It ended with unconditional surrender for one of the parties. This illustrates some of the criteria we want to convey: the symbol of total war, of "absolute war," and its counterpart in the form of the more limited war.

Focusing on wars in Europe in the early modern and modern era, it seems that the large wars arrived about 100 years apart. The outbreaks of total warfare have 100-year, mostly peaceful breaks, interludes. The great wars have a duration of roughly thirty years, as we see here:

> The Renaissance War, 1494-1527
> The Thirty Years' War, 1618-1648
> The Coalition Wars, 1792-1815
> The World War, 1914-1945

There are three aspects to investigate. The length of the wars (about thirty years), the intervals (about 100 years), and what characterizes these wars, their "total" nature.

2. Length of Total Wars and Intervals

Firstly, the length of the wars requires examination. The duration of the Thirty Years' War is self-explanatory. For its part, the Renaissance War (a label we're applying here) is fairly in line with this, lasting for 33 years. The Coalition Wars are usually not seen as *one* war, rather they are traditionally known as the Revolution and Napoleonic Wars, respectively, but everyone understands that they belong together. When unified into a single war, it becomes a 23-year period, which fits the overall pattern.

Finally, the World War had its long period of peace in the middle, lasting twenty years. This might be an anomaly in the context. However, this peace period was nibbled at from one side by the Russian Civil War, lasting 1918-22, and from the other side by the Spanish Civil War in 1936-39. The stock market crash in 1929 also led to a period of *structural violence* (unemployment, civil unrest), triggered by the war economy and other factors. We're probably not the first to see the First and Second World War as a single, conjoined 31-year war.

These intervals are followed by 100 year (circa) intermediate periods of relative peace. For example, between the Renaissance and the Thirty Years' War it's 91 years, which is not far from the mark. Between the Thirty Years' War and the Coalition Wars, the interval is 144 years, which is longer in duration. However, the interval between the Coalition Wars and World War is 99 years, so the median value becomes 99 years.

3. Specificities

Concerning the specifics of the "great" wars and their "total" character, we will commence with the "Renaissance War." To begin with, the French king Charles VIII is said to have surprised the Italians when he marched on Italy in 1494 with hostile intent.

The Frenchmen stormed the cities and took prisoners, which was previously unknown in the maneuver-style warfare of the *condottiere*. But the Italians quickly learned the language of total war.[26] Italy became the scene of a long and bloody war over who would rule Europe; this was far more than a game of cabinet politics. Major battles were fought in Ravenna 1512, Novara 1513, and Marignano 1515. The greatest battle of the century was at Pavia in 1525. The end of the war was marked by the Sack of Rome in 1527. The Treaty of Cambrai in 1529 formally terminated it, called the "Peace of the Ladies," because women conducted the negotiations.

After Pavia, significant, pitched battles became very rare. According to Montgomery,[27] Ceresole 1554 and Nieuport 1600 were the only exceptions. This can be interpreted that Europe was wartorn and entering a phase of maneuver war and calm deliberations. But, as always, the power struggle continued: who would rule Europe? At the time, it was France against the Empire and Valois versus Habsburg. Overall, however, the period after the Renaissance War was peaceful; in so far as if one waged war, it wasn't *total* war.

The Thirty Years' War was a violation of this trend. Again, the warfare became total. The armies grew: for example, Wallenstein's first army counted 150,000 men, the largest army Germany had ever seen.[28] Cities were taken and set on fire; the last time Italy was ravaged, now it was Germany. The troops lived off the land, harrowing Germany like locusts. Art was stolen, with the Swedish sack of Prague being a symbolic event for this war. In characterizing this war, you could also think of this line: "With the mild blessing of God captured in the war," a sentence that Kluge cites concerning the family fortune of a certain "General von Ha." The war referred to is expressly said to be the Thirty Years' War.

---

[26]   Montgomery, 1970, p. 212.

[27]   Ibid, p. 222.

[28]   Weibull, 1962, p. 94.

4. Westphalian Peace and After

The Thirty Years' War concluded with the Peace of Westphalia. Furthermore, the immediately subsequent wars often ended with the status quo according to this war. Sweden was, for example, one of the guarantors of the Westphalian Peace; our participation in both the Swedish-Brandenburg War and the Seven Years' War took place based on this, that we would play our old role of guarantor of the Peace of Westphalia. The status quo of the Thirty Years' War should be preserved. This war was the emblematic, incomparable war of the time; it was "the Great War" of its era.

In other words, after 1648, we again saw a phase of limited war, characterized by armies exercising some restraint in plundering or not plundering at all. As such, art was seldom looted. According to Boberg (1985), the tactics of the 1700s were overwhelmingly defensive. Decisive battles were avoided, and maneuvering became the order of the day. Military stockpiling replaced systematic plunder; the movements of the armies were planned based on storage bases. An army shouldn't be more than five days' march from a base, but new bases took time to build. This kind of pre-planned stockpiling resulted in the civilian population being, in principle, spared from plunder.

Specifically, during this time, it can be said that a commander like Marlborough fought hard and well — but not brutally. Moritz of Saxony (1696-1750) was one commander who argued that you could win a war mainly by maneuvering and thereby virtually avoiding fighting.[29] This was possible as Europe was war-torn after the Thirty Years' War — this was an interval between two periods of total war. From this angle, all of these are Wars of Succession (the Palatinate, Spanish, Polish, Austrian) and the Seven Years' War. For example, Prussia seemed to be on its last leg at the end of the latter, but the Great Powers didn't unite to eradicate it with fire and sword. It seems that during this era, there's a gentleman's agreement, consciously or

---

[29] Beaufre, 1966, p. 58.

not, to keep the wars limited. Calm deliberations with small steps were the prevailing style in warfare and politics. Europe, during this interval, was subconsciously haunted by the ghost of the Thirty Years' War and doing what it could to avoid it.

This small-scale policy collapsed when the French Republic flooded Europe with its armies in the late 1700s. Again, it led to total war. It was a war of plunder and devastation, symbolized by Napoleon's marching without a baggage train. According to Wallenstein, armies above a certain size feed themselves. Once again, the looting of art became common during these coalition wars. The looting of art as a phenomenon will be discussed in greater detail later in this chapter.

One significant event in this brutal zeitgeist occurred when the French entered Lübeck in 1806 and exposed the city to *three days of plunder.* Three days — this is quite a lot. *"Cry havoc and let slip the dogs of war...!"* Among other things, a house belonging to Friedrich Philipp Victor von Moltke, father of the later famous Helmuth von Moltke, the victor at Sedan 1870, was ravaged.[30]

Thus, again, it's a state of total war. All the resources of the French nation are focused on the war. In 1793, mass conscription inflated the French Republic army to one million men. And if the enemy couldn't be defeated, it could be crushed economically. This is another thing characterizing the total war. Can you imagine, for example, the Austrian War of Succession with a pan-European embargo, citizen armies, and a war minister Carnot working day and night to organize the country at war? No, you can't because the Austrian War of Succession was a limited war. The Revolutionary War was total.

One refined quote of these years was the opinion of the English statesman Pitt after Austerlitz: "Roll up that map; it will not be wanted these ten years." This symbolizes a situation of "Europe in the crucible, throw cool deliberation out the window" — which is typical of the total war atmosphere.

---

[30]   Moltke.

Typical, also, for eras of total war is the tendency to produce "*Nicias Peaces.*" A Nicias Peace means a settlement, in retrospect, lasting only for a limited time. The term is from the Peloponnese War. Thus, "Nicias Peaces" during the Coalition Wars were, in our eyes, all those entered into between 1797 and 1809: Campo Formio, Lunéville, Amiens, Tilsit, and Schönbrunn.

5. And So...

With the Congress of Vienna in 1815, a new epoch began, which was mainly peaceful, and the wars that were fought were once again limited. Of course, Prussia's battles in 1864-71 were total enough for that country — but — countries not involved in the conflict expressly abstained from intervening. There was a tacit consensus of not wanting an all-European war again. The specter of the Coalition Wars still haunted the recent past, it now playing the virtual role of "the Great War you don't want to let loose again."

The Crimean War and the Franco-Austrian War also had a kind of 18th-century flavor, according to Alf W. Johansson [1994], as did the Prussian wars of unification, with their "cabinet-style, limited-war" approach, such as the deliberations of the diplomatic game, with most maneuvers favoring Bismarck. The fact that no victory parade was held in Vienna in 1866 and that the one held in Paris in 1871 was relatively small occurred on Bismarck's insistence. Bismarck was no "total warrior." He wanted to limit the lingering hard feelings, and this era did allow one to rein in the everyday expressions of "dominance and submission" prevalent after a victory. In short, it was a time of limited war. Again, such was the sentiment due to the collective subconscious having the Coalition Wars in an all-too fresh memory. No one wanted the total, all-European war back.

The time after 1815 is reminiscent of the period after 1945 — not surprisingly, since they are *isochronous* and are at the same position in the cycle with an atmosphere of "after Actium": two blocks of

41

power emerging, an Eastern and a Western, now, after 1815, with Russia, Prussia, and Austria in the former camp, and England and France in the latter. There is a certain resemblance to the east and west of the Cold War, which was also a time of limited war. Post-1945 is "after Actium," remember...![31] Louis Philippe, inspired by Talleyrand, approached England and *voilà*, an "*Entente Cordiale*" in anything but name came true. Then the two powers went their separate ways, without becoming outright enemies, until 1904 when they entered the historical Entente Cordiale. Russia, Austria, and Prussia can be considered as a conservative alliance until 1850.

In 1914 the total war broke out again. "The lamps are going out all over Europe, we shall not see them lit again in our lifetime," Lord Grey rightfully said. The war lasted for more than four years; it lasted for 31 years. Versailles was, after all, "not peace, it's an armistice for 20 years," as Ferdinand Foch stated.

In other words, Versailles was a Nicias Peace. Yet another striking indication of this is a cartoon from the times concerned. The four greats who dictated the peace, Lloyd George, Woodrow Wilson, V. E. Orlando, and Clemenceau, were depicted in the following manner. They "come out of the session hall and see a boy crying in a corner." Clemenceau says, "Curious, I seem to hear a child weeping!" The boy has "1940 class" written above him, meaning that in twenty years, he will be called up as a soldier for a new war thanks to the rigidity of the peace since it was a mere temporary solution. The title of the drawing is "Peace and Future Cannon Fodder," published in the British paper *Daily Herald* on 13 May 1919.

Versailles was a temporary settlement in a period of total war. Despite the peace, Germany didn't accept the role of the eternally defeated. It still wanted hegemonic power in Europe, and therefore started the war incrementally (Rhineland, Sudetenland, Czechoslovakia, Poland), just as it had stopped incrementally in 1918-1922. With time, the United States and England decided to

---

[31]   For details about the intimated 19th century block policy, see Andolf, 1976, p. 106.

resist Germany and see its "unconditional surrender," something they certainly have been criticized for — how brutal...! However, historically, it's somewhat natural to fight for the enemy's unconditional surrender when a total war is fought. The Peloponnese War ended similarly; the Sparta-led alliance forced Athens to unconditional capitulation.

After 1945, peace has mainly prevailed in Europe. Occurring conflicts were fought in a limited way, with no camp having mobilized all their military might and brought it to bear. One example, perhaps extreme, would be that NATO didn't use nuclear weapons when it intervened in Yugoslavia. Nor were they used in Vietnam or Iraq, even though they reportedly threatened to use them in the latter conflict. In general, regarding the situation post-1945, that old, familiar war-weariness has prevailed; no regime, either in the East or the West, has been able to mobilize the population to total war dimensions. This is important when looking at the post-1945 era — in Europe and worldwide.

After 2011-2012, a major war became impossible. We elaborated upon this in *Actionism*.[32] Following 1990 the war trend decreases. Libya 2011 was the last old-school invasion, the last remotely "major" war. Furthermore, we have the esoteric indicia of 2011-2012 as a period of transition provided by Calleman (2004) and McKenna (*q.v.* the phenomenon "Timewave Zero"). The current zeitgeist is against a significant war erupting. So, as far as we can see, the above pattern of war cycles, solid as it is when looking at the past, probably can't be applied to predict the future.

6. Cyclical Approach

Fredrik the Great said that conditions might be similar but rarely identical in the history of war. This was about the art of war per se, the fighting itself, the art of winning pitched battles. However, the

---

[32] Svensson, L., *Actionism*, (Australia: Manticore Press, 2017).

same tendency applies to the history of war in the broader sense, seeing some strains return without identical conditions.

This can be a rule of thumb when the cyclical approach is applied. The total wars discussed above *resemble each other* but *aren't identical,* just as the long intervals of peace resemble each other without being identical. In that case, you could say that history is cyclical, not in the sense that everything returns automatically, but in so far as the development is moving forward in a spiral rotation. For example, the time after 1945 resembles the time after 1815; however, the course of the intermediate 130 years can't be ignored. Chronologically, 1945 isn't the same point in time as 1815.

Few historians seem inclined toward any kind of cyclical view of history. Instead, with variants, *the linear eschatological model* is in use, where everything develops linearly and incrementally toward some obscure culmination, whether it is seen as a disaster or a paradise. If you are of a Leftist disposition, you tend to see things bright, and everything is getting better. But if you have a Rightist disposition, you tend to see things darker, everything heading for a major *Untergang*. However, the linear view is common to both. The cyclic approach is nonexistent today; it's perceived as a nullity and absurdity among mainstream researchers.

Linearity is the *leitkultur*. And therefore, so few can see the similarities between the "predominantly peaceful intervals," like those of 1648-1792 and 1815-1914. Instead, to explain the similarities, they grab at ad hoc explanations — such as the peaceful atmosphere of the former period being defined by the charitable effect of the ideas of the Enlightenment. In contrast, the same atmosphere of the latter is explained with the Congress of Vienna, the Holy Alliance, and the "European Concert." But then, as it happens, you can also see the Enlightenment ideas employed to explain the brutality of the Coalition Wars...!

Conversely, to describe the peace periods after the Thirty Years' Wars and the Coalition Wars as war-weariness, a consciousness of the scourge of total war, and a tacit willingness to prevent this have never been encountered in the literature at hand. You may catch a glimpse of it, as in Alf W. Johansson's *Europas krig,* but it never dominates. Even Clausewitz in *On War* ignores it; he duly noted the break in zeitgeist between the central part of the 1700s, the French revolution, and the Napoleonic era, but he fails to see the same interval between the late 1500s, early 1600s, and the outbreak of The Thirty Years' War. Again, this is because of the limitations of the linear approach. A scholar using the linear method can't apply the same explanation for two distinct but similar periods since the linear approach to everything is *evolving,* changing, and becoming irreversibly different over time.

Yet another example of using ad hoc explanations in the absence of cyclical clarity is how to explain the occurrence of the looting of art. For instance, it has been said that art looting in the Thirty Years' War were due to the regiments being recruited and paid by the commanders themselves, not by the state. But during the Coalition Wars, even though the state set up the regiments, it surely didn't prevent them from looting, with the French army as an example. In the 1790s, the actual government *ordered* Napoleon to rob Italy of its art. In mainstream history cases, you may find other explanations for art looting, such as the influence of revolutionary ideas. However, to say that in both cases (looting of art in the Thirty Years' War *and* the Coalition Wars), it was due to the total war reversal of the customs. The fundamental "disruption of the social fabric" is something which usually remains unconsidered.

7. Looting of Art

Before concluding, let's take a closer look at the *looting of art.* Perhaps this can highlight the complex phenomenon of total war. In summation and chronological order, consider these factors.

Sweden freely plundered the Empire in the final stages of the Thirty Years' War in connection with the storming of Prague. Books such as the Silver Bible (now on display in Uppsala University library) and the bronze statues that adorn Drottningholm Palace Park today were taken.

During the 18th century wars, according to Boberg [1985], there was little looting of art and literature. Artistically minded princes bought their items instead of stealing them. Frederick the Great invaded Dresden twice but left the art collections intact. Russians and Austrians who penetrated Berlin in 1760 also left its artifacts alone.

On the other hand, the Coalition Wars saw a new level in the looting of art. Napoleon, a "trendsetter" for the style, waged war in Italy in 1795-99 on the French Republic's instigation. In addition to squeezing money out of the Italian states in the form of "contributions," many *objets d'art* and manuscripts were taken to Paris. According to Boberg (1973), Napoleon expressly received orders from the French government ("the Directorate") to do so. The Louvre Museum of Art became the storehouse for many of these objects. France was forced to return many of them after 1815. This is said to be one of the few points in the peace talks where Talleyrand disagreed with Wellington.

As for the looting style of the Napoleonic Wars, you can read it in Dumrath (1899). "The war should feed the war," was the common knowledge. The operational style of the French army wasn't about having storage bases or paying for provisions. Plunder was considered to be the soldier's right. So the army looted, officers looted, and soldiers looted. In this atmosphere, even generals were allowed to take their share, including the theft of art. One example of this is Marshal Soult, who gathered some artifacts when he was Andalusian proconsul, including Murillo's Madonna, which he then sold to the Louvre for a reasonable sum.

Nazi Germany looted art during World War II and returned it after 1945. Russia also took some art from Germany in 1945 as informal damages, such as the "amber room" of Prussian fame.

8. Ares and Athena

In ancient times, the Peloponnesian War between Sparta and Athens was fought. It lasted 431-404 BCE (27 years). It was a total war of the kind we have previously discussed, incorporating elements such as the desolation of rural areas (economic warfare), demagogues, devastated cities, and general resentment. It concluded with the unconditional surrender for Athens. As such, a devastating 30-year-war is not just a phenomenon of the modern age.

The focus has been on the time from the Renaissance through the 20th century and discerning its cycles of war. However, an investigation of veritable war cycles in antiquity could also be done. There were other total wars in addition to the Peloponnesian war. The First and Second Punic Wars, the "Mediterranean War" 168-133, and the Civil War 49-31 had some elements of a total war. We have already mentioned the trope "after Actium," referring to the naval battle ending the Civil War and inaugurating the era of Pax Romana. In 1945, Ernst Jünger appropriately wrote in his diary that we are now "after Actium." It's the sensation of an epoch passing, a time of total war coming to its end.

The Peloponnese War is useful as a template for total war. After a couple of years of fighting in the Peloponnesian War, Sparta and Athens made peace, brokered by the Athenian statesman Nicias. But the peace didn't last. It only turned out to be provisional. In that case, concerning European wars, the Amiens peace and Versailles peace were typical Nicias Peaces.

Finally, a mythological reflection can be made regarding antiquity. If we say that the total war has a revolutionary character, that it's a war of the kind that "destroys the game," a battle that lives its own life, this can be said to be a war in the spirit of *Ares*. This God was responsible for the unruly, disorganized battle — while *Pallas Athena* was responsible for the organized, regular battle. For preparation and planning in war, it's *her* war you want: limited war, strategy, transparency — and not the total war of Ares, which is devastating war, the destruction of armies, and changing history.

Time of Total War

- "Ares" war
- "Break and bend" (Clausewitz)
- Looting of art
- Economic warfare

A peace concluded within such a period tending to be a Nicias Peace. Ending with an "after Actium" atmosphere and an attitude of "*vae victis.*"

Time of Limited War

- "Pallas Athena" war
- "Observe and negotiate" (Clausewitz)
- Warfare as "the art of maneuvering"
- The armies pay for their necessities
- Reduction of the size of armies
- Begins with an "after Actium" atmosphere

III. ANECDOTES

In 1762 French philosopher Rousseau said of Corsica: "I have a premonition that someday this little island will astonish Europe." Seven years later, Napoleon was born there.

*****

Richard Lionheart is known as an English king. But he only spoke French.

*****

When King Alfred of Wessex visited Rome, he was given the title of "roman consul," 400 years after the fall of the Roman Empire.

Speaking of the longevity of Roman titles: whether he's historical or not, Rome's founder Romulus adopted the title of Pontifex Maximus, *great builder of bridges*. Today, almost 3,000 years later, the Pope of Rome carries the same title.

*****

"What price, Churchill?" — In 1939, after Churchill once again had failed in his efforts to enter the government, posters with this text were seen in central London. It's still not known who was responsible for the posters.

*****

During the so-called Moscow trials in the Soviet Union during the 1930s, this once happened: one of the accused confessed to having met Trotsky for a conspiratorial meeting at Hotel Bristol in Copenhagen. Soon, however, it was found out that this hotel had been torn down already in 1917.

*****

The medals for the Victoria Cross are still made of bronze from cannons, taken at Sevastopol during the Crimean War.

*****

When the Duke of Wellington (the victor of Waterloo) was buried, it took over an hour to read out his titles.

*****

WWII, unusual enemies: The British sinking French ships at Mers-el-Kebir, 1940. And the British fighting the French in the Syria-Lebanon campaign of 1941.

WWI, unusual allies: After the Japanese surrender in 1945, the British used the Japanese as auxiliary units to fight the Indonesian guerrilla.

IV. MONARCHS

1. Alexander

A king is a man doing kingly things. A king is a king is a king... The depiction of monarchs, kings, and other crowned heads in Western history is a vast undertaking. We will begin with Alexander, one of the most mythical kings of antiquity, indeed, even in the entire history of the world.

In antiquity, people deliberated over whether Alexander was essentially good or bad. The eulogies may have predominated, but he did have some lowly deeds on his account. For example, when his friend Hephaistion had a fever, the doctor ordinated a strict diet but being a sturdy Macedonian, he couldn't abstain from a breakfast of fowl and a jug of wine one day. His fever rose quickly, and soon he was dead.

Alexander went out of his mind and had the innocent doctor killed. True story? It was told by Plutarch, who otherwise paints a heroic picture of the man.[33] Therefore this could be a stain on the Alexandrian armor. However, he will remain a legend even because of this. One foul deed doesn't drag a man down into villainy. Compare this to King Arthur's actions, who slaughtered innocent children to kill the one who was said to overthrow him one day.[34] No one has stopped admiring Arthur because of this. It's a grave

---

[33] *Life of Alexander*, which is the source of this and the following anecdotes.

[34] *Le Morte d'Arthur*, Book One, Chapter 27.

episode, but figures like these can't be regarded in a *binary* fashion, that is, right or wrong.

Neither Alexander nor Arthur can be labeled either all good or all bad. Primarily, they were both humans. However, in their activity as rulers, they weren't always saintly.

*****

Once during a party, Alexander had an argument with general Cleitus, who criticized him for being haughty. Tempers were running high, but the others succeeded in separating the two, and Cleitus was persuaded by friends to go to bed. However, soon he returned through a side door and said something pithy; Alexander then took a spear from one of his bodyguards and pierced Cleitus with it. To kill an adjunct when drunk is hardly praiseworthy, but in Alexander's defense, it must be said that he regretted it afterward. The following night and day, he stayed in his quarters crying. However, the situation of Alexander drinking wasn't rare. He could do it for hours upon end and then spend the next day hungover. Plutarch tells us this, although he tries to smooth it over.

Alexander was capable of cruelty. During the Indian campaign, some captive mercenaries had been promised free lease but were later attacked and killed, *hors de combat*. Then there was the rebellion of Thebes before the Persian campaign; it was struck down, its citizens were sold as slaves, and the city was razed to the ground. Enslaving captives in this way may have been common practice then; however, annihilating a city wasn't. The Thebes incident can be seen as an outrageous act, and even Alexander himself is said to have regretted it afterward, like trying to treat a Theban mildly whenever he met one.

*****

These were accusations made against Alexander that questioned his honor. What about the praise, though? Did he deserve his epithet "the great"?

Of course he did. For instance, he didn't spare himself in the battles he fought. However, a commander shouldn't always be in the thick of battle. He should be a *focal point* so that he can *lead*. All told, Alexander won many battles, and that's what counts for a commander. He won them squarely. This is illustrated by the anecdote of him seeing the Persian army camped before Gaugamela but refusing to attack it in the dark, *not wanting to steal his victory*. This is a royal, noble attitude.

Continuing in this vein, his father Philip was proud over the victories his horse equipage had won in the Olympic Games. When Alexander's friends asked if he would compete there, he just said:

I would, if I could compete against kings...

Alexander was, for that matter, not wholly against athletics and sports; he staged them as often as he could, but to compete in them was beneath his dignity. This is a far cry from some Roman Emperors, like Nero's performance as a *quadriga* driver and Commodus' muscular posing before the cheering crowd.

In Corinth, when Alexander met Diogenes, who lay basking in the sun, he gently asked Diogenes if he could do anything for him and received the snide comment to move because he was obscuring the sun. However, Alexander was impressed by this free spirit and afterward said to his companions:

You may say what you want, but if I weren't Alexander, I would have liked to be Diogenes...

In other words, Alexander could put his role as a ruler in perspective. On the other end of the scale, he was impressed by the Persian ruler Cyrus' tomb, which he encountered in Pasargadae on the way back from India. On this mausoleum was engraved:

O ánthrope, egô Kyros eimi; tên archên tois pérsais kéktemai, tês de Asías bebasílevka. Mê oun fthonêsês moi tou mnêmatos. O man, I am Cyrus who founded the Persian kingdom and ruled over Asia. Do not grudge me my monument.

The mausoleum was a small stone building on a relatively high fundament, with a saddle roof and a narrow entrance. Alexander only found a gold chest and a divan with gold feet inside. However, originally there had been a splendid cover for the divan on which were placed tunics, Median jackets and pants, robes colored in amethyst and purple, necklaces, sabers, jewelry, and other *objets d'art*. It had been plundered when Alexander got there, but he restored the house to its former glory. The mausoleum itself is still there, but all content has been gone for a long time.

2. Young God

When marching against the Persian Empire, Alexander was young, merely 23. He won victory upon victory. In Egypt he visited an oracle belonging to the god Zeus-Ammon, who greeted him as his son. Exactly what this meant has been discussed rather widely. Perhaps the oracle said "my son" to all who came there, but Alexander interpreted it all literally: "I am the son of god..." Alexander gained the whole Great Kingdom with all its riches when the Persians were utterly defeated at Gaugamela. He was greeted by his Asian subjects with traditional genuflection, the face to the earth, and all that. The Persians didn't regard their kings as gods, but Alexander must nonetheless accept such greetings. He must do it as an emperor; that it upset his fellow Macedonians is another matter.

He was the Lord of the World or believed himself to be, ruling the whole Middle East in addition to Greece, and received messengers from various small civilizations like Romans, Scythians, and Carthaginians. This was his empire, and regarding other countries, India hadn't been fully explored, and the Greeks didn't even know that China existed. Alexander was king of the world at thirty and appointed god by an oracle. The philosopher Anaxarchos also informed Alexander that everything a king does is right; no wonder he started to leave the ground and soar. There arose a strain of arrogance in him, a lack of measure, of *mêtron*. When India had to be conquered, his men refused to follow him, and he dejectedly returned to Mesopotamia, the core of the kingdom. Once there, Alexander planned new campaigns, including sailing around Africa, but death caught up to him first.

Alexander's goal was to make war, and if one campaign ended, a new one would follow. On the other hand, he never conceived of a political foundation for his conquests. The reason for the Persian campaign might simply have been revenge for the Persian War one and a half centuries ago. This is open to speculation, but a great ruler must be a little more than just a warrior, which Alexander sometimes seems to be reduced to being. He attacks the Persian kingdom and defeats it — and what did he do then? Well, now it's about bringing the Persian man to justice who killed Darius during his flight; in one fell swoop, Alexander, the aggressor, turned into the protector of the Persian Empire. Eventually, this Bessus is caught, but the campaign goes on, encountering satrap after satrap, each one receiving the standing message of continuing in his office unless he has misbehaved, in which case he would be replaced.

Alexander didn't create anything new. He only ran along already paved lanes, making a victorious tour of the Persian Empire and consolidating what Cyrus and his successors once built. Not even the Indus Valley had been left unscathed by these Persian empire builders. Punjab, for example, was conquered by Darius the Great sometime before 500 BCE. However, Alexander's path is still impressive. His ride through the Khyber Pass in command of a Greek-Persian army of over 30,000 men is an immortal vision, a position that no other westerner achieved during ancient times. But in essence, Alexander tends to be nothing more than a continuation of the line of Persian kings, let alone a legendary one. Alexander didn't change the Middle East; the Middle East changed him.

3. The Surrender of Kings

Alexander fought his last major battle against King Porus in India. Porus was defeated, but Arrian only had praise for him. Despite the battle turning against him, he didn't escape like Darius at Gaugamela. Instead, he continued to fight as long as his units still stood. Only when he was wounded, did he turn the elephant on which he rode and retreat. Later he met Alexander; the latter held his horse and looked admiringly at his opponent, for his countenance was full of pride. "His expression," Arrian writes, "was that of a brave man who meets another, that of a king in the presence of a king with whom he fought honorably for his kingdom."

Alexander asked Porus what he could do for him.

"Treat me as a king ought," said Porus.[35]

Alexander agreed to this but asked if there was anything special he wanted. "Everything," said Porus, "is contained in this one request."[36] This is reminiscent of Kipling:

> East is east, and west is west,
> and never the twain shall meet,
> until earth and sky stand presently at
> God's great judgment seat.
> But there is nor east nor west,
> nor blood, nor breed nor birth,
> when two brave men stand face to face,
> 'though they come from the ends of the earth.

It can also make you think of the saying that anyone can win, but only a gentleman knows how to lose; only he can do it with dignity. Perhaps this is the ultimate touchstone for the behavior of a king, for a king to show that he's a *king*. The behavior of Porus is outstanding in this manner, but there are certainly more memorable

---

[35] Arrian, p. 281.

[36] Ibid.

royal capitulations in ancient times. The most famous example occurred when Lydia's king Croesus surrendered to Cyrus; the former, according to Herodotus's first book, had just taken place on a bonfire where he would be burned when he twice called out the name "Solon." Cyrus held back the ignition and asked who this Solon was, and Croesus replied that this was a wise man who had told him that you couldn't be called happy until you die. Croesus hadn't then understood what Solon meant since Croesus was rich and powerful at the time, but now he understood the entire essence of the wisdom.

Croesus was pardoned and then became an excellent adviser to Cyrus in his continued conquests in the Middle East. At the time of the surrender, in the capital of Lydia, Croesus provided sound advice; the Persian soldiers were burning down the city, but Croesus said to Cyrus that this was stupid because they devastated their own property, for the country was theirs once victory was obtained. Cyrus took note of this advice and put a halt to the burning. This is similar to Alexander's burning of the Persian royal palace in Persepolis. According to Plutarch, most historians agree that he quickly regretted it and put the fire out, probably for the same reason as Cyrus at Sardes. This also reminds us of the Red guardsmen who stormed the Winter Palace and began to plunder it. According to John Reed (*Ten Days That Shook the World*, 1919), they ceased doing so because someone in the unit proclaimed that this was the property of the people now.

There is another example of "surrendering kings" found in Herodotus' Book Three, concerning Cambyses. Cambyses, a successor of Cyrus, had conquered Egypt, and wishing to humiliate King Psammenitus, had his daughter dressed as a slave and brought before him with other noble girls, carrying water. The other Egyptian dignitaries began crying at the sight of this, but Psammenitus said nothing, simply gazing at the ground in silence. Then a companion of the king's son and two thousand others were displayed to him, with bridles around the mouths and bound by ropes. Again, Psammenitus was impassive.

Then an old acquaintance of Psammenitus happened to stroll past, one who used to eat at his table but had now become a beggar. At the sight of this, Psammenitus burst into tears. 'Why?' asked the king. Psammenitus replied that his grief at the sight of daughter and son was too great for tears, but he was powerless to hold back tears at the sight of an old friend losing his wealth and becoming a beggar. This was reported to Cambyses, who was moved by the event and began to treat Psammenitus well. However, Psammenitus later planned a rebellion, it was discovered, and he had to drink a cup of ox blood. He died on the spot.

There is also Perseus' surrender after the third Macedonian War. The Romans were victorious at Pydna, which led to the invasion of Macedonia and eventually the capture of its king. Dressed in dark clothes and accompanied by his son, he was brought before the Romans, who were proud and astonished by this spectacle — for it was one of the most outstanding achievements Rome had ever won — the capture of a ruler embodying the grandeur of Philip and Alexander the Great.

When Perseus was presented to the consul, the Romans asked why he started the war, for the Romans just wished him well...? But Perseus just stared down at the ground and cried. Then the consul again asked why he had chosen enmity with the Romans, so strong in war and magnanimous in peace. Again, the answer was silence. This response was appropriate, for it is debatable why the Romans actually went to war with Macedonia this time and if it really was a *bellum justum*. The silence of Perseus is an excellent demonstration of royal splendor, even in defeat.

4. Rome and Its Kings

The Romans defeated Perseus, which compels us to describe this people's attitude towards royalty. It's well known that the early city-state of Rome was ruled by kings and followed by a rebellion that toppled the kingship and inaugurated a republic. The Roman *style* then became a belief that the "republic" stood for everything that was good and "monarchy" for all that was bad. The Roman Republic may be worthy of praise. Still, it must be noted that it retained some royal relics, such as the ivory-adorned tribunal *sella curulis,* used by consuls and other senior officials, the title *interrex* ("middle king") for interim rulers, and *rex sacrorum* for a particular civil servant, which means "king of the sacrifice."[37]

However, if a republic was good and a monarchy was bad, how did the Romans establish an Empire, which is a monarchy in its highest power? They *did* establish it, but many conceptual pains accompanied it all. This shouldn't obscure the fact that monarchy was on its way long before it was established around year 0. We had, for example, Sulla, who was a dictator for ten years in the 80s BCE; against current practice, he made this military office for emergencies into a permanent office. And with his regime of violence, he may have been the first to give the title a bad name.

This didn't deter Caesar from appointing himself dictator for life one generation later. Rome still had a republic, but it was on its last leg because, for example, all elections for the public offices were rigged; people with money could achieve whatever they desired with bribes, and street fights customarily accompanied the polls. Even the senate nobility had begun to get the drift, having for a while supported Pompey and transforming him into a sort of single ruler. They appointed him as sole consul, contrary to the custom of the office being a diarchy, and being a consul gave him such extensive powers (to fight piracy in the Mediterranean, and also "responsibility for grain supply" with powers over all maritime traffic and coastal provinces of the Empire) that he was virtually a monarch. But he lost the civil war against Caesar, who thus allowed himself to be appointed dictator for life.

The situation was delicate. True, Caesar may have managed to attract many former enemies. However, it was feared that he would

---

[37]   Bjöl & Hjortsö.

appoint himself *king*, the worst thing imaginable to the Romans of that era. So it was taboo; after the last Etruscan king was toppled, a republic was seen as the root of all goodness, and kingship was the root of evil.

The symbol of the kingdom was a *diadem*, a kind of headband, which was offered to Caesar by Mark Anthony during an official ceremony. Plutarch (*Life of Caesar*) tells us that when Caesar rejected the diadem, it was met with applause. However, afterward, Caesar was dissatisfied with the performance, and it would have been better not to stage it whatsoever. But something had to be done to placate the masses. It wasn't sufficient for Caesar to say, "I am not king, I am Caesar…."

The Romans disliked kingdoms and monarchy — in principle, it seemed taboo. It would take a long time before this was changed, and it required the governing skills of Augustus and Tiberius for the Empire and the Emperor to be deemed acceptable by the societal elite. Their talent disguised the fact that the new governance was essentially a monarchy. And *voilà*, by the time of the Antonine Emperors, the *empire* was generally considered the best governance ever.

5. *"Kingdom Without Royal Insignia."*

Caesar was suspected of tyrannical aspirations, which led to a conspiracy, ending in his murder in the year 44 BCE. But Caesar's case was avenged by the adopted son Octavian (the future Augustus), who understood better than his father what was appropriate for Rome's political culture. After defeating Caesar's murderers and later Antony, the former ally, he did everything to reduce his role; he never appointed himself dictator, never even whispered the word "king" (*rex*), and merely called himself "the first of the Senate" (*princeps senatus*), taking on the office as a people's tribunal. The senate nobility cheered, now the Republic had been restored...! But keen observers may have noted that now there was a new kind of monarchy, a "kingdom without royal insignia," in the expression of Suetonius, which would mean having a king without the diadem used by the ancient kings of Rome. According to Suetonius, Augustus himself is said to have wondered if he shouldn't reintroduce the Republic, withdrawing entirely from his position of power. Still, he could not do this without the whole Empire being engulfed by chaos.

There was a monarchy, an autocracy, an empire, but it was not yet fully established — for instance, the inauguration of Tiberius' rule. Here Tacitus depicts Tiberius sitting in the senate attended by the senators, asking him to pick up Augustus's fallen mantle and rule like him, but Tiberius is hesitant. In the end, he utters the memorable words, "I will not say yes, but I'll refuse to say no." It's doubtful that similar scenes occurred in any other great empire of the time (China, India, Persia). It is unlikely that a designated ruler would appear reluctant to assume the monarchial office while pretending that the monarchy itself is something despicable and needs to be abolished.

At the same time, the Tiberius episode reveals something valuable in Rome's political tradition: the effort of defining what a particular position of power means, the very discipline of *constitutional law*, a discipline that is probably something typical of the Western world. In other empires, the king was simply a king and relatively unproblematic. However, this excludes China, where Confucian thinkers queried how rulers should act, resulting in the principle that rebellion against a bad emperor was allowed. In India, the *Arthaśāstra* focused on practical politics and *Realpolitik*. The Indian ideal of a ruler in *Dharmaśāstra* was of a more holy, elevated character. So, all told, we doubt that you could find a better example than that of Cicero, who stated that Roman governance was a *monarchia mixta*, a form of government blending traits of democracy (popular assemblies), aristocracy (the senate), and monarchy (the consuls). This presents a fine example of constitutional law.

6. Roman Emperors

Regarding Roman Emperors, there are several inspirational figures. However, after reading Suetonius, we can quickly dismiss Claudius from this list. Claudius was made famous in the contemporary era by Robert Graves's novels and the TV series based on them. Graves did consult Suetonius, but then he created an idealized portrait. The historical Claudius is no ideal but rather a half-mad parody of a ruler who enjoyed torture and was influenced by his wife and advisors.

For example, when acting as a judge, a prime function of the Emperor, according to Suetonius, Claudius' sentences were often too harsh or too mild, resulting in complete arbitrariness. As for his cruelty, Claudius liked to watch torture and executions. At gladiator games, he ordered the killing of gladiators, especially of so-called *retiarius* (a fighter equipped with a trident and a net), even though they had just been tripping and falling, *so that he could see their faces at the moment of death.* And when a particular gladiator duo died, Claudius ordered that their swords should be taken and made into little knives for him. This is far from the kind and friendly Claudius we saw in Derek Jacobi's screen interpretation, where the pitiful, stuttering little man only wanted to read classics but was forced into Realpolitik because of his ancestry.

In terms of foreign policy, Claudius is praised for completing the conquest of England that Caesar began, but in geopolitics, this is deemed a mistake. The main effort had been the conquest of Germany, but they realized it could not be done, and the Elbe border was unattainable. Therefore, the Empire had to look for easier gains to obtain more plunder, triumph ceremonies, and endless victory celebrations. Claudius chose Britain instead and received what he desired: glory as a triumphant commander and the adulation of the people. But the conquest per se couldn't have yielded much because of having to station troops there instead of on the German border, where they were needed more. Britain was a strategic dead-end. The Empire wasn't threatened by this remote island and should therefore have left it to its own devices before coming to grips with the German threat — which it never did — so the taking of Britain was a wild goose chase, a futile goal-in-itself, a vane yearning after *gloria militaris.*

Still, Claudius had one or two redeeming features. He was a comparatively gentle emperor compared to Caligula before him and Nero after him. There weren't so many excesses under Claudius, no sex orgies, and no purely moronic undertakings. At his peak, Claudius was akin to a *bonus pater familias,* which was not the worst approach for an emperor. For example, there is the Suetonius anecdote when Claudius at the Circus had freed a gladiator from further service because his four sons had prayed for him. Claudius immediately sent for a writing board with a message in which he reminded the people of how important it was to have children because they could serve as help and protection even for a gladiator.

Thus, Claudius' regime is framed by Caligula and Nero. Of the former it can be said that he was probably already a little mad even when young and that he just made one memorable uttering, showing his interest in murdering people: "I wish that humanity had only one neck!" As if he wanted to say, "*I'm crazy, and I know it...*" His rule had his fair share of debauchery and murder. It was the same with Nero, but he seems to have been relatively sound at the beginning of his government. His musical side will be explored in Chapter Five, in an attempt to restore his reputation. Among his other laudable aspects, we find his building projects. Rightfully, he disliked the random jumble that Rome was. The streets were too narrow, and the spread of the buildings was a hard-to-survey conglomeration due to organic growth since the founding of the city. However, Nero took it a bit too far in his planned renovations, resulting in more destruction than he initially intended. There is also the famous image of Nero playing the harp and singing of the destruction of Troy while Rome burns. However, this may be a myth. Later, the grand palace Nero built, his Golden House, was torn down by a successor who built the Colosseum on this site.

Nero had his moments, such as playing with the idea of abandoning Britain and realizing that the above-intimated strain of it was a dead end. This would save money — but — as Suetonius says, he didn't do it out of fear of dishonoring his father's name, that is, Claudius, who had adopted him and made the conquest in the first place. It was "politically impossible" to retreat from Britain, which is an argument against the island being taken at all.

In 68 CE, Nero faced a severe rebellion and was forced to flee Rome. He was in a villa when his adversaries caught up with him, prompting him to recite: "Hoof-beat sound in the ear from fast-paced horses..." which is a line from the *Iliad*. Then, assisted by an aide, he thrust a knife into his throat and died when a centurion came rushing in. Thus Nero (as some historian said), in his last moments of terror and humiliation, displayed some courage and determination, leaving the scene for the last time, but without applause.

Of the three Emperors who ruled in 69 CE, only Galba stands out. There are different versions of events mentioned by Suetonius, and the best is when Galba is pursued down Rome's streets but finally gives up, urging the attackers to "do their duty and stab, because this is your will." It was a death befitting a king if the episode is factual.

Vespasian came to power following a coup, ending the political chaos of 69 CE. However, he hadn't started the coup himself but was pushed to the highest levels of power by various garrisons who wanted him as emperor. Concerning his government, there's nothing else to say than that for better or worse, he was a *bonus pater familias*: good for the Empire, bad for scandal-mongers. He was succeeded by Titus, who, it has been said, didn't even rule long enough to earn a bad reputation. Domitian, who followed him, received a worsened result. Regarding Domitian, we will say nothing more than reciting this fine image from Suetonius: before going to bed, Domitian used to "take a walk by himself in a secluded place." This is a gripping image of the ruler as a private man, a human being strolling in a garden and looking up at the moon before deciding it's time to hit the sack.

7. Look the Part

If you intend to be a monarch, you should look the part and possess a majestic countenance. Ironically, Caesar, in this regard, wasn't so lucky. It was not that he was ugly — but — as Plutarch says, he was "a slightly built man, had soft and white skin, suffered from headaches and was subject to epileptic fits."[38] This was an obvious disadvantage for a military commander, so Caesar had to train his physique to withstand the requirements of life in the field.

Caesar's primary opponent in the civil war, Pompey, was more blessed concerning his physical appearance. According to Plutarch, Pompey was charming, possessing "a kind of dignity and sweetness of disposition," and further that:

> [...] at the height and flower of his youthful beauty there was apparent at the same time the majesty and the kingliness of his nature. His hair swept back in a kind of wave from the forehead and the configuration of his face around the eyes gave him a melting look.[39]

Pompey wasn't really "Alexandrian" in appearance (as some then considered him to be). However, like Alexander, Pompey also deserves the epithet "the Great." One can study the facial expressions of Pompey and Caesar by examining their sculptured busts. Pompey comes across as a satisfied man, having had his fill of victories, while the face of Caesar exudes a strong will to power, a man still striving for glory.

Pompey was also a blunt military ruler unable to use even the barest form of rhetoric — for example, when he and Crassus agreed to become consuls in 70 CE, the senate questioned them. Pompey replied that the answer might be yes or maybe no, and when pressed for a better solution, he said that he wanted to get votes from the

---

[38]   *Fall of the Roman Republic*, p. 260.

[39]   Ibid, p. 158.

Republic's good elements, not it's terrible. Thus, as Plutarch states in his Crassus biography, Pompey left an impression of arrogance. At the same time, Crassus, with his answer to the question — that he would stand for office in the consular election if it were in Rome's interest — was better at interpreting the sentiment at hand. Another example occurred when Caesar inquired if Pompey would defend a specific law, and he said, "Of course, and if anyone begins to speak of swords, I can provide both swords and shields." Everyone admitted that this was a stupid statement from Pompey, overly hasty and unnecessary. Caesar, for his part, didn't seem to make such blunt statements probably because he had studied rhetoric as a young man. Pompey had, from his youth, learned the soldier's trade and was devoid of an educational polish.

A passage in Suetonius' biography on Caesar illustrates Caesar's rhetorical prowess and Pompey's lack of skill with rhetoric. When dealing with the parties in the Civil War, Pompey declared that he would consider those who would not fight for the Republic as enemies, while Caesar announced that those who were neutral and didn't support any of the parties would be counted as friends. This clearly shows the diplomatic talent of Caesar, which was necessary to heal the wounds of the Civil War.

In other words, Caesar showed a lot of mildness (*clementia*) during and after the Civil War. For example, he pardoned Brutus, who later thanked him for his gratitude by killing him. Furthermore, Caesar tried to mend and ameliorate the divisive Roman situation. Suetonius seems to understand this, but then he rebukes Caesar for receiving too many honors, ruling with dictates, and having a sharp tongue at times. The last point is worth mentioning because it is an aspect often ignored. For instance, according to Suetonius, Caesar celebrated a triumph after returning to Rome when the Civil War was over. As he passed by the tribunes, one tribune — Pontius Aquila — refused to rise, whereby Caesar exclaimed, "Try to take the Republic away from me, then, Aquila!"

A hasty remark doesn't transform Caesar into a lowly villain. On the contrary, it makes him endearingly human. Even accounting for the accusations of Suetonius' biography, the text as a whole is a portrait of moderation and grandeur. Suetonius is a bit more candid than Plutarch, but, all told, these two biographies don't turn the reader into a Caesar hater.

At the same time, we have to admit that Caesar is a kind of rebel, not an elevated majesty. He strives for the monarchical seat, but he doesn't possess it from birth like Alexander. Specifically, we must state that Caesar was a careerist. For example, on his way to his office as governor of Spain, he passed a small town, and someone in the company said what an 'appallingly desolate burgh' this was. According to Plutarch, Caesar replied, "As far as I'm concerned, I would rather be the first man here than the second in Rome."[40] Pompey never wrote anything similar, and he was nobler with his accounts.

Caesar was a *Streber*, striving to be important, unable to play a waiting game, and not subscribing to the principle "everything comes to the one who waits" nor the Taoist, "do nothing, and everything shall be done." He crossed the Rubicon and seized the state; he resorted to violence (or, instead, the threat of violence) to open the treasury, which is a fact that could be held against him. A tribune called Metellus refused to grant Caesar access to the treasury because it was against the law; Caesar then stated that "it's war now and then there's no room for law." One wonders what a man with Pompey's regal charisma would have done in the same position.

It was a war, and Caesar had entered Italy with his legions, contrary to the law, having crossed the Rubicon, which designated the boundary of the demilitarized zone that existed to prevent precisely such a march against Rome. Pompey had moved south with his units and brought the majority of the Senate with him. It was an exodus for society's elite. In any case, Caesar had to resort to a threat of violence concerning the treasury. He did get it opened, and the leading figures that remained in Rome, having feared his

---

[40]   *Fall of the Roman Republic*, p. 255.

arrival, began to soften their attitude toward him; it was the power of *clementia*, the statesmanship of Caesar, his very magnanimity, winning them over. This was followed by his battle against Pompey at Pharsalus, Pompey's flight to Egypt (where he was murdered), Caesar's arrival in Egypt and his romance with Cleopatra, the Battle of Zela (with its *"veni, vidi, vici"),* various victorious battles, and the conspiracy and assassination of Caesar in the Curia, which resulted in his death beside a statue of Pompey. Finally, it culminated with a royal funeral decorated with gold and purple.

8. Fox and Lion

Caesar was avenged by his adopted son Octavian who completed what he began. The Republic was abolished, step by step, but in forms that made people believe it survived. But what can we say concerning Octavian's — who was later known as Augustus ("the elevated") — leadership? Georg Brandes, for his part, related that Augustus was a "fox" that reaped everything that Caesar, "the lion," had sowed. Caesar was great by nature, and Augustus was fake and cruel by nature.

It is true in that Caesar struggled with a more-or-less open visor while Augustus was a born politician, a sly fellow "taking all means and pathways, if they led forward." Augustus was undoubtedly talented, though. He created a political system that, honed by Tiberius, could be left in the hand of mediocre rulers without the Empire falling apart in the process.

Suetonius provides a critique of Augustus. Augustus was appointed a god after his death, and how could you attack a god without being accused of blasphemy? Perhaps Suetonius and other critics took refuge in true Roman casuistry. For a while, the Emperor was cultivated as a veritable divinity in the eastern part of the Empire. In the west, they only worshiped his *genius*, his protective spirit. Therefore, you could criticize Augustus the Great.

One of Augustus' negative traits mentioned by Suetonius is that he sometimes executed prisoners of war who had asked for mercy. As for his positive aspects, Suetonius claims that when punishing rebellious tribes, the worst that Augustus resorted to was selling the people as slaves, thus implying that he didn't kill them or raze their cities to the ground. If you compare this to what Alexander did at Thebes (who sold the population as slaves and then razed the city), one gains an insight into what was considered *harsh and cruel* or *decent and mild* in the international affairs of the ancient world.

Augustus coined some intriguing phrases. He had mottos like "hurry slowly" (*festina lente*), "a cautious general is better than a bold," and "what's done well is done fast enough." When Augustus was on his deathbed, he said: "Applaud, my friends!" (*plaudite, amici*), as if he wanted to say that life is just a performance and being a monarch even more so. This expressed an attitude of distancing yourself from a leadership role, akin to Alexander's statement that he would have preferred to be Diogenes if he had the freedom of choice.

It is also of interest that Augustus had considered reintroducing the Republic. But, according to Suetonius, he didn't because he wouldn't feel safe if he retired as a private person and that the state would also fare badly. Ultimately, Suetonius praised Augustus because he left matters as they were — in this era, the "empire" was one of the finest things imaginable.

Tiberius followed Augustus. According to Suetonius, Augustus had weighed his disadvantages and merits against each other and found that the latter predominated. The same verdict can be reached by reading Suetonius' biography and Tacitus' *Annals* I-VI. The latter source is a bit tendentious, for everything that Tiberius says and does in the spirit of the amateur psychologist is interpreted in the negative. Sometimes even Tiberius' silence is interpreted to his disadvantage; he mulls on evil thoughts, as Tacitus tells us.

In comparison, Augustus was pleasant enough to deal with, ruling like a benevolent father, the *bonus pater familia*, while

Tiberius was a strange type, "an unsmiling, unlovable man," who eventually settled on the island of Capri and ruled the Empire from there. All of this was bad for his reputation, spawning gossip and slander in the aristocracy, who wondered what their Emperor was doing on this island. According to Suetonius, there are various peccadilloes mentioned in the case of Tiberius which have not been questioned. Tiberius was a convincing, powerful Emperor, but there is a distinction between the individual and the ruler. Tiberius could be seen as a bad ruler, but as a royal *gestalt,* the Tiberian governance doesn't provide one much to oppose. On the contrary, Ernst Jünger, in his novel *Eumeswil* narrates a favorable image of Tiberius.

So, why does Tacitus criticize Tiberius? During the reign of Tiberius, there were often accusations of *lese majesty* — treason. Tacitus says that treason was committed against the Roman people, in the beginning, attacking its *maiestas* (dignity, reputation) — such as betraying armies, invigorating the people, and, finally, by the inept handling of an office. Actions, not words, were punishable.[41] For example, Augustus referred to the publication of pamphlets as treason, and Tiberius continued to do this. Thus *words* (directed against the Emperor) also became a criminal offense. However, according to the Annals, no one was convicted for treason during the early reign of Tiberius. It was often on the initiative of others that someone was charged with this, while the Emperor tended to dismiss the charges and pardon the accused. Then, in the wake of Sejanus' coup attempt, many were convicted on charges of treason, but this was an exception. The state was in danger, and many were dreaming of reintroducing the Republic — and how fortunate would that have been. Did they really want the late Republic back with its mob rule, bribe, and civil war...?

All told, Tiberius was a relatively good monarch. For example, in his speech in Book Three of the *Annals,* Tiberius speaks of the impossibility of legislating against luxury, which seems to be the epitome of insight and moderation. Preventing luxury and excess

---

[41]　Tacitus, *Annals,* Book I.

might be desirable, but Tiberius realized where the limits of politics existed on this issue. Politics is "the art of the possible." In terms of geostrategy, Tiberius was always active in securing the northern boundary of the kingdom against the Germans. In general, this operation became a half-measure, and the solution reached (the Rhine-Danube border) was the only one possible in this context. In any case, Tiberius' actions are worth noting. Compare his sense of duty and seriousness with the fool Caligula, the clown Nero, and the half-mad Claudius.

Details aside, Tiberius seems to have been a decent emperor. He, Augustus, and Caesar created the Roman Empire, which remained even under unimpressive Caligula, Claudius, Nero, and 'The Year of the Three Emperors' mildly suspect types. However, one should not overpraise Tiberius. He *had* dark aspects to his personality — and it wasn't surprising that people were happy when he died because by then, many bodies had gathered at the foot of the Gemonian Stairs, the victims of suspicions of conspiracy, both real or imagined.

When Tiberius disappeared, the Romans were happy. But when Caligula took the throne, this changed.

Tiberius had the gift of oratory like Augustus. For example, he once said that you should only shear your sheep, not flay them regarding a proposal to raise the tax. Another example of Tiberius' rhetorical skills can be found in an anecdote by Suetonius.

> Once when a funeral train passed by, a joker came and loudly addressed the dead, telling him to say to Augustus that the gifts he had bequeathed to the Roman people yet hadn't been paid out. Tiberius then ordered the man to be brought to him and repeat what he had said to the dead, and then be executed so that he could give Augustus the message in question.

This episode describes Tiberius in a nutshell: brilliant and cruel at the same time.

9. Barbarian Chieftain

In *De Bello Gallico* Caesar provides an account of the conquest of Gallia, now known as France. Details aside, it's very readable. In addition to pitched battles against Gauls, there are encounters with Germans and two outings to the British Isles. The end of the text deals with a Gallic rebellion, the climax being the siege of Alesia, where the Romans have encircled this city with a siege wall. A rebel army operated from outside, and to protect themselves, the Romans were forced to construct another wall parallel to the siege wall. They were between a rock and a hard place. The army proceeded to attack, and those in Alesia seem to be venturing an outbreak — but then the Germanic cavalry in Roman service is inserted against the outer army, striking it and stabilizing the situation. The beleaguered Gallic force in Alesia surrenders, and the whole Gallic campaign has reached a successful conclusion.

Leader of the uprising was the Gaul Vercingetorix, and his capitulation is described as follows by Plutarch:

> Vercingetorix [...] put on his most beautiful armor, had his horse carefully groomed, and rode out through the gates. Caesar was sitting down and Vercingetorix, after riding round him in a circle, leaped down from his horse, stripped off his armor, and sat at Caesar's feet silent and motionless until he was taken away under arrest, a prisoner reserved for the triumph.[42]

Plutarch embellishes the scene. The account by Caesar, who was there, describes himself sitting on the siege wall, then Vercingetorix was brought before him, and his weapons were thrown on the ground.

However, that wasn't the end of the story for Vercingetorix. A note in the Swedish version of *De Bello Gallico* states that Vercingetorix

---

[42]   Plutarch, *Fall of the Roman Republic*, p. 271.

was held prisoner until 46 BC and was exhibited as part of the triumphal procession, after which he was executed in secrecy. This is criminal, regardless of whether Caesar himself ordered the murder or someone else did it. You deserve ethical treatment if you have surrendered because if your surrender only leads to execution, it's meaningless. You might as well end the final battle with a kamikaze attack, dying a truly royal death and becoming a legend.

It was cruel, but you must admit that it was also efficient and fitted the style of Roman sobriety. They knew how to consolidate their gains, how to build an empire that would endure. Furthermore, there were no Gallic rebellions after Alesia. Compare this to the actions of Alexander, who let Porus live and continue to rule after his surrender. This *laissez-faire* policy simply wasn't appropriate for empire building. Alexander didn't consolidate his gains. He just kept on making war. He fought too much and politicized too little.

10. The Limits of Power

Vercingetorix was a barbarian chieftain, and overall, they didn't wield much power. For example, Tacitus' *Germania* (Chapter Seven) states that the German kings did not possess unlimited or arbitrary power. A similar statement is found in *De Bello Gallico*: "In times of peace there is no common government; instead, the local leaders of larger or smaller settlements administer justice and settle disputes." However, in times of war, it was different: "When a tribe wages a war, chieftains are chosen to lead this war with unlimited power over life and death." (Book Six)

The same phenomenon is seen among the Gauls, where in Caesar's Book One, a Haeduan chief says that his people are divided into two camps, one of which is serving the enemy, but he saw no way of mastering them. Thus, he's a chief lacking more acute means of ruling and has no coercive power. He might have exerted symbolic and even judicial control but could not expressly force anyone to do anything. He was relatively powerless. There are similar examples in Book Five where Ambiorix, the chief of the Carnuts, had difficulty settling under Roman rule. When asked about this, he said that it was the people who more-or-less forced him to act as he did: "His power was of such a nature that the majority of the people had as much power over him as he over the people."

However, the power of the Gallic kings would have increased in war. Returning to the rebel leader Vercingetorix, in Book Seven, it's said that as the leader of the Gallic army, at one point he procured grain, "and he laid down the death penalty for those who didn't obey." In this regard, Vercingetorix was more powerful than another rebel leader, Washington, who had no coercive powers to resort to when his army was starving, and the peasants wouldn't give him grain. That was the situation for the rebel army at the turn of the year 1779-80.

As for Vercingetorix's leadership qualities, the following can be said. In the year 52 BCE, the Gauls rebelled against the Roman rule established by Caesar a few years earlier. The Romans had taken some rebellious strongholds, and Vercingetorix advocated the burning of farms and villages to obstruct the provisioning of the Romans because defending them would be more difficult. But the people of Avaricum (Bourges) didn't want to burn their city. This was the most beautiful city of Gaul, both a bastion and a pride for the people. They tried to defend it, but Vercingetorix soon acquiesced because of the prayers of the Biturigians.

The Biturigians defended their city, but the Romans finally took it; Vercingetorix was nearby with his army but couldn't prevent it. Later he held a meeting to limit the damage suffered: the Romans hadn't won with superior bravery or in open conflict, Vercingetorix said, but through warfare and skillful siege, which was something they lacked experience with. It would be erroneous to expect constant success in a war. Vercingetorix had opposed the defense of Avaricum, but now he would attempt to remedy this situation with new ventures, for instance, inciting the whole of Gaul to rebel.

Caesar comments on this by saying that the speech by Vercingetorix made an impression because he had not lost courage, despite the setback, and he had not retired or retreated in the eyes of the public. Also, he possessed the ability to anticipate upcoming events – like the situation at Avaricum. The authority of military leaders is often lessened by defeat, but for Vercingetorix it increased instead (Book Seven).

Vercingetorix grasped the nettle and turned the situation around: he was a fine example of a king and a Responsible Man. The episode also highlights the futility of holding on to and defending cities in war. For instance, in 480 BCE, Athens was abandoned on Themistocles' advice, it wasn't popular, but nonetheless, the people decided to follow the advice, evacuating to the island of Salamis and making sure that the navy was ready for combat, which in the ensuing battle triumphed and won the war. A similar episode occurred when American rebels abandoned Philadelphia and let the English occupy it without this becoming critical to the war at large. The Russians also abandoned Moscow in 1812, and Napoleon captured a major city without winning anything. This illustrates the fact that the operations of war aren't always primarily enacted to defend or conquer the land, but simply to defeat the enemy's units. This was observed by Frederick the Great and then adopted by Clausewitz in his book *On War*.

Finally, there is the Haeduan chief, Dumnorix, whom Caesar (in Book Five) held hostage. The Romans attempted to force Dumnorix to accompany them on the expedition to Britain. But Dumnorix stalls, saying that his religion doesn't allow sea voyages, and eventually, he escapes. Caesar pursued him with a cavalry unit, and Dumnorix was killed. His last words were, "I am a free man of a free people!" This statement appears historically accurate, for Caesar has no reason to fabricate this declaration. The episode may illustrate chieftains' sovereignty and pride, preferring to die in freedom than become a slave of Rome.

11. *Greece*

The Greek concept of royalty was unique. According to Furuhagen, during Mycenean times, the title for a king was *wanax*, under which lesser kings operated who were called *basileis* (singular, *basileus*). When the Mycenean kingdoms fell, these *basileies*, with time, became top leaders in the new, smaller realms, the city-states. However, these *basileis* weren't very powerful kings; they seem to have only been *primus inter pares* in ancient aristocratic states. Then a new form of rulers called *tyrants* appeared, named after a Lydian word that meant "king," and these tended to be more influential, often coming to power with the help of mercenary troops. They reformed the city-states and gave more significant influence to the freeborn people, the *demos*. These tyrants eventually became corrupt and were overthrown, and thus democracy became the order of the day. While this was the case in Athens, it was not in Corinth, which was the first tyrannical state. After Corinth ended its tyranny, an oligarchy with a people's assembly created a new political landscape. However, some tyrants continued to rule in the Greek world, for example, Sicily c.300 BCE. For instance, Plato's dealings with the tyrant of Sicily are well-known, and his writings on the subject lead to the bad reputation the word "tyrant" now holds. On a side note, Jünger in *Eumeswil* has a different interpretation of the Greek tyrant.

Historically, the concept of a tyrant is not such a moot point anymore. Most historians admit their role as vanguards of a new era. The tyrants of c.500 BCE were a kind of Renaissance *condottieri* or "Rienzi-style tribunes," breaking the power of the nobility, basing their power on the bourgeoisie, and favoring art and culture. Martin Persson Nilsson states that the tyrant Peisistratus laid the foundation for the grandeur of Athens because Attica wasn't very significant — it was only a backwater, a remote corner of the Hellenic world. Therefore, from a historical point of view, the tyrants were monarchs, and like most monarchs, their dynasties were good at the beginning and then gradually deteriorated. Apart from the later Platonic critique, the word "tyrant" received some of its bad reputation from Hippias, the last Athenian tyrant.

Athens abolished its monarchy in favor of a republic similar to that of Rome about the same time — but unlike the Romans, the royalty wasn't so taboo to the Greeks. For example, during the resistance against Macedonia, Demosthenes was crowned, and before this, Alcibiades received the same honor for victories against the Peloponnesians. In the case of Alcibiades, the word was out that he should have become a dictator (Plutarch's choice of words), but no murmurs of dissatisfaction were expressed by the mass of spectators when Alcibiades was crowned, which occurred when Caesar seemed about to be crowned by Mark Antony. The royal insignia wasn't so forbidden in Athens, regardless of its republican tradition.

12. Demetrius

They say that Alexander was more upset when someone refused a gift than when someone asked for a gift. This demonstrates *generosity* as a royal trait. Another illustration of this phenomenon is found in Plutarch's biography of Demetrius, the son of the Diadoch ruler Antigonus who, at the end of 300 BCE, fought against the Egyptian ruler Ptolemy. Antigonus' army operated in Syria under the command of Demetrius, who was only 22 years, and this was the run-up to his first pitched battle against Ptolemy. The battle was fought at the city of Gaza, in Syrian territory.

Demetrius, however, was no match for someone like Ptolemy, who attended Alexander's school of war. Demetrius lost thousands of men, who were either dead or captured. He even lost his tent, wardrobe, and all his personal belongings. But Ptolemy returned these to him and nobly said "that they didn't fight for life and death but only for glory and power." Demetrius gratefully received the gifts while praying to the gods that he would soon be able to repay this generosity. It came sooner rather than later, for the Ptolemean

General Cilles arrived in Syria. He didn't pay much attention to Demetrius, and in the battle that took place, the latter won a complete victory. The Egyptian army was routed, and Demetrius took its camp, including 7,000 prisoners and various booty. He, of course, was delighted with this victory, less for the honor and all the spoils of war that it brought than enabling him to return the generosity of Ptolemy. Cilles was overwhelmed with gifts and sent back to his ruler.

Later, Demetrius became the king of Macedonia, but he wasn't a perfect king. The following anecdote was mentioned in Chapter One, and here it is in a more elaborate form: once, when Demetrius was out walking the streets of Pella, people presented him with petitions — but after receiving the documents, he threw them into a river in plain sight. Later, he was approached by an old lady who asked for a hearing, but Demetrius replied that he had no time. Then the woman shouted at him, "Then don't be king!" According to Plutarch,[43] this gave Demetrius food for thought. He immediately returned home, stopped everything he had planned to do, and gave audiences to anyone who wanted one for several days, starting with the old woman. In other words, a resounding call from the depths of the people had made him realize what it meant to be a king.

Demetrius was the first Greek ruler to appoint himself king after the death of Alexander. The great realm Alexander left behind was divided. When he died, a series of wars followed, with the Diadochi to determine what realms would arise in the process. One of them became Macedonia, where Demetrius then made himself king after defeating Ptolemy's navy at Salamis, where he was crowned with a diadem. Soon, Ptolemy, Lysimachos, and Seleukos were also crowned kings of Egypt, Thrace, and the Middle East. However, Seleukos had already accepted royal insignia when he gave audience to the Persians and other Orientals.

But everything still wasn't all peace and happiness, because Plutarch adds that the adoption of the king's name was something

---

[43] *The Age of Alexander*, p. 372.

more than a formality to these men; it spurred their ambitions, made them think differently and enabled them to be proud and arrogant, just like an actor changes his pose when wearing royal garb. As a consequence, they also became stricter in their judicial rulings.

Of Demetrius' appearance, Plutarch writes:

> [...] there was something intensely theatrical about Demetrius. He possessed an elaborate wardrobe of hats and cloaks, broad-brimmed hats with double mitres and robes of purple interwoven with gold, while his feet were clad in shoes of the richest purple felt embroidered with gold. One of his robes had taken many months to weave on the looms: it was a superb piece of work in which the world and the heavenly bodies were represented. It was still only half finished at the time of Demetrius' downfall, and none of the later kings of Macedonia ever presumed to wear it, although several of them had a taste for pomp and ceremony.[44]

The same source records another great anecdote of Demetrius. After having conquered Megara and taken a lot of spoils, he said to one of its citizens, "I leave this a city of free men!" The man retorted:

> You may say that indeed, for you have not left a single one of our slaves.[45]

13. Warrior Kings

Demetrius and Pyrrhus were warrior kings, and all the other monarchs in this chapter have had a connection with war. Alexander warred and won battles like no other. Caesar was a daring campaigner during the Gallic War, the Civil War, and the fighting in Egypt and Sela. Tiberius had been living the soldier's life on the German border

---

[44]   Ibid, p. 371-372.

[45]   Ibid, p. 343.

before becoming Emperor. Augustus had a somewhat more limited soldier career. However, it's well known that his most important role was as the commander of armed forces. The following Emperors all lived under pressure to distinguish themselves as field commanders, which resulted in ridiculous exercises like the military outings of Caligula and Nero.

The tyrants of ancient Greece were closely associated with the rule of the sword. They based their power on mercenaries or the lower citizenship armed as heavy infantry (*hoplites*). Therefore, monarchs are closely associated with war, soldiers, and military might. Another example of this is in the Old Testament. After the Jews migrated to the Levant and established their kingdom, they were ruled by men with long beards, called *judges*. Eventually, this reaches a point when it's no longer feasible, and the nation wants a king. However, Judge Samuel isn't keen on this idea, and when talking to God, he, God, decides that *he* is the king of the Jews.

Nevertheless, if they want a king, they shall have one. Samuel is advised to read the law to the people concerning the actions of a king, such as taxes, etc. This culminates with the congregation stating that they want a king as a war leader: "[...] with a king to lead us and to go out before us and fight our battles."[46]

The role of the king in warfare was probably the main reason to establish a kingdom. The people of Israel had long engaged in warfare, fighting against Philistines and others to obtain their Promised Land. The best way to do so was to appoint a king, a warrior who was also given "residual powers" over the people and functioning as an executive political leader. At the same time, the judges remained as priests and spiritual leaders.

Kings and war belong together. However, the ancient *republics* — such as the Roman Republic and Athens in the Persian Wars — were also proficient in warfare.

Saul was the first Jewish king and was followed by David, and both successfully expanded the kingdom. However, the greatest Jewish

---

[46]   1 Sam. 8:20.

king was Solomon. Solomon built the temple for the glory of God, a temple that would not be of iron. Instead, copper should be used as iron was for weapons. Therefore, Solomon had a more peaceful reign. War was something that his predecessor David had engaged in. Therefore, because David had blood on his hands, he could not build the temple, and this task had to be performed by Solomon.

Solomon was wise and presided over a golden age. According to the First Book of Kings, Solomon was the wisest man who lived, and "[...] from all nations people came to listen to Solomon's wisdom, sent by all the kings of the world, who had heard of his wisdom."[47] As a result, the Kingdom of Solomon overflowed with gold to such an extent that silver was deemed worthless in his day.

14. Generosity

Previously we spoke of generosity as a royal trait. Demetrius was one example of a generous ruler. Alexander also demonstrates generosity in his dealings with the Indian King Porus. A similar, early modern case would be Sweden's Charles XII. Voltaire writes that he conquered crowns only to give them away. Charles gave away the Polish crown to Leszczinsky because he wasn't interested in it for himself.

There are other instances where Charles demonstrates great generosity. First, before the war, he lavished gifts on his sister and her husband, the Duke of Holstein, as part of the marriage festivities. Also, during his stay in Turkey, Charles freely handed out gifts and bribes.

This was not just about bestowing gifts and wishing to gain approval from doing it. Beyond the atmosphere of *voluptas* (largesse, opulence, and abundance), the rationale for kingly generosity was to make the receiver of the gift dependent on him. *Do ut des:* I give so that you shall give.

---

[47]   1st Kings 4:34.

15. The Tomb as Royal Symbol

Earlier, we mentioned how impressed Alexander was when he saw the tomb of Cyrus in Pasargadae. The power of the royal grave enables us to culminate the discussion of "the role of the monarch." Symbolically this anchors the subject of "the monarch" in our current era, too, not just antiquity.

Royal power has a mystical dimension, and the enduring symbol of this magic is the royal grave.

For instance, in June 1940, after the fall of France, Hitler toured Paris and visited the tomb of Napoleon, a rotunda with the actual sepulcher in the center, partially submerged so that one could gaze into its depth. The sight visibly moved Hitler. He later said, "The moment in Paris where I saluted Napoleon's tomb was one of the proudest of my life."

Moreover, Napoleon had also visited the royal grave of Frederick the Great in Prussia. Reportedly, Napoleon was so obsessed by the memory of this great commander and king, although he had defeated Prussia in 1806 at Jena and Auerstädt. Therefore, Napoleon had to go to the *Garnisonkirche* in Potsdam to see the actual *tomba* in the church vault.

This was a meditative respite for a man of power, enveloped in monarchical mysticism, symbolized by the grave.

Previously, in 1805, Alexander I of Russia also visited the tomb of Frederick when he was in Prussia to summon the fortitude required against Napoleon. Several artworks depict him in the vault by the tomb with the Prussian king Frederick William III and his wife, Louise.

Similarly, the Potsdam church, which contains the tomb, was visited by the Third Reich on 21 March 1933 (*Tag von Potsdam*). Following ceremonies in the church hall with Hitler, Hindenburg, and various dignitaries, Hindenburg went down into the burial vault alone to exert a ceremonial presence in front of Frederick's tomb.

Hindenburg was chosen for this because, as a child, he had known his grandmother's gardener, a man having served seven days under Frederick.[48]

This is a striking example of historical continuity, which has been elevated to a mythical level by the power of the royal grave.

Ending on a less fateful note, we see the same phenomenon — a European monarch performing a ritual by a royal grave — when Swedish king Carl XIV Johan visited the burial mounds at Uppsala in 1834. Starting as "Jean Baptiste Bernadotte," he had become king through suspicious means, so his legitimacy was a bit shaky, to say the least. However, the Uppsala ceremony, attended by crowds and the usual dignitaries, may have given Carl some sorely needed symbolical credibility as a monarch of the Swedes. The power of the earth mounds, the resting place of early iron age rulers, exuded their invisible yet tangible spiritual power, the mystique of the monarch *in nuce*.

---

[48] Kluge, Schlachtbeschreibung.

V. MUSICAL RULERS

Q*ualis artifex pereo:* "what an artist the world is losing in me." These were the last words of Nero, a seeming example of arrogant presumption. Perhaps he made a fool of himself by performing on stage as a reciter of poems to the sound of the *kithara*. According to Suetonius, Nero didn't have much of a singing voice. However, the same historian says that Nero had a talent for writing poetry early on and that he had a genuine interest in poetry and sculpture.

Therefore, with reservations, Nero is qualified as a musical ruler — a ruler with a keen eye for culture, a ruler with some contact with the Muses, the gods of poetry, song, and art. This is no mere pastime, for sometimes, art may guide politics. Exploring this concept throughout the ages might reveal some unusual perspectives on political history. Accordingly, we will first explore antiquity before proceeding to the New Era and the Faustian world.

Nero was an emperor of the Julio-Claudian dynasty, founded by Augustus. Augustus had earned a reputation as an enemy of culture by banishing the poet Ovid from Rome because of his supposedly pornographic *Ars Amatoris*. This instruction in the art of seducing a woman might seem relatively innocent today. However, for the Roman mentality, that of responsible empire builders, it was inappropriate to Augustus. However, he was not ignoring the doings of his own family in this respect, such as banishing his daughter from Rome due to immoral behavior.

Nevertheless, Augustus was no barbarian and not entirely blind to the cultural side of life. If he couldn't sleep (according to Suetonius), he had a reader or a teller of histories to entertain him. He also wrote several works: an autobiography (still preserved), a metric poem about Sicily, and a tragedy concerning Ajax, the latter of which was never completed and destroyed because he didn't like it.

Another culturally gifted emperor of this dynasty was Claudius. Suetonius states that he wrote several historical works, including a history of the Etruscans. Unfortunately, all these works are now lost. However, as intimated earlier, as an emperor, Claudius was mediocre (due to tactics such as invading the geopolitical dead-end of Britain), and he had a personal penchant for cruelty. This is all in Suetonius' accounts. The image of Claudius in Graves's novel (and the TV series based on it) is a misleading whitewash when examined from a purely historical perspective.

*****

Alexander the Great had a favorable disposition towards culture and music. He ruled with an iron rod, true, like raising Thebes in 334 — but — he expressly wanted to save the house of Pindar. So a sign was posted on his house saying:

> *Pindárou tou mousopoiou tên stégên mê kaíete.*
> Do not burn down the house of the poet Pindar.

Alexander often honored the gods with games and dithyrambic choirs, such as at his return to Phoenicia from Egypt. Plutarch records this. In Arrian, it is written that Alexander was on his way home from India when as a thanksgiving for crossing the Gedrosian desert, he staged a festival with games including both athletics and cultural subjects. A similar event was also held in 330 BCE when Alexander honored his dead friend Hephaestion in Ekbatana. Again, competitions in both literature and athletics took place at the funeral.

86

Plutarch also states that Alexander always brought a copy of the *Iliad* on campaigns. Believing it to be the supreme handbook in the art of war, Alexander always kept it under his pillow along with a dagger. Once, when campaigning in a remote part of the Middle East and having nothing to read, a helper presented him with tragedies by Aeschylus, Sophocles, Euripides, Sicilian history by Philistus, and dithyrambic poems by two poets named Telestes and Philoxenus.

*****

Returning to Rome, there is the case of Marius, a vigorous general of simple origin, whose career was dedicated solely to the craft of war. He never studied Greek literature and never used the Greek language in a meaningful context. Furthermore, he considered it ridiculous to study literature composed of subjugated people. When Marius attended the temple's consecration that presented a Greek theater performance, he briefly entered the theater, sat down for a moment, and then left. Plutarch, the source of this information, adds that if Marius had honored the Muses, he would have lived a better life and not become a victim of his ambitions, passions, and greed. This might be true, but Marius's enemy in the Civil War, Sulla, had some musical leaning, which hardly made him a better person. With mob rule and proscription lists, Sulla ruled Rome just as cruelly as Marius did. Sulla was reminiscent of Nero: interested in culture but also cruel.

Sulla was far from angelic in disposition, but his musical strain makes him more complex than Marius. Sulla, for instance, socialized with people involved in the theater. However, according to Plutarch, Sulla couldn't take anything seriously as soon as he had sat down at the dinner table.

*****

87

Caesar wasn't so overly cultural, although he had some redeeming features. He could write. However, the identity of the author who actually wrote *The Gallic War* and *The Civil War*, with the author name "Julius Caesar" on them, is open to debate. It certainly isn't impossible for a general to write a concise narrative of his career. In the contemporary era, Douglas MacArthur has done the same. In his youth, Caesar studied rhetoric in Cyprus under the same teacher that taught Cicero. Caesar's rival Pompey had no such schooling, and it showed. As previously discussed, he could be indelicate and did not possess the same ability to "sell" his politics as Caesar had.

*****

The greatest Athenian statesmen, both with an ability to govern and accompany the Muses, are Pericles and Cimon.

According to Plutarch, Pericles knew the musician Damonides. Damonides had formalized the Greek metric system and expressly stated that music can't develop without political changes (a more noble view would be that culture and the Muses should lead society instead of being dependent on political situations). Cimon sang at a party once in his youth, after the libations had been poured. He was praised as a more remarkable man than Themistocles, whom he succeeded as the ruler of Athens. However, he did become greater than the victor of Thermopylae, for Themistocles was eventually banished and died as a Persian provincial governor. Cimon was also banished, but he returned and remained an Athenian for the rest of his life, dying as an honored statesman in his native land.

*****

The fact that Cimon could sing well is reminiscent of Tsarist Russia, where the ability to play an instrument was considered a favorable trait for a state official. When applying for a higher office (general, governor), playing a musical instrument was considered a merit.

For example, Frederick the Great could play the flute. The Danish King Christian IV also had the lutist John Dowland in his household orchestra, paying him a salary similar to that of a general.

Furthermore, the *Amadis* novels inspired the Spaniards to seek cities in the New World — and they found Tenochtitlan and Cuzco. This is a prime example of culture guiding politics.

*****

Harald Fairhair of Norway had many a good man in his entourage. Some he sent out on missions, others always accompanied him, like the poet Olve Hnuva, "because of his gift as a poet." This is found in *The Saga of Egil*, which is about an Icelandic chieftain of the 900s, Egil Skallagrimsson. Egil himself was a fine illustration of "cultural interest in a man of action" and of "unity of power and spirit." He was a Viking who visited royal courts, composed songs of praise and was compensated for this, but he also went to war and participated in various adventurous excursions. He was a poet and a warrior in one.

One European ruler who took his cultural interests even further was Ludwig II of Bavaria, who built dream-like castles with fantastic architecture, both with and without Wagnerian inspiration. The buildings possessed enduring construction, and the state of Bavaria is generating profit on what it once paid to construct the castles. In the 21st century, tourists are enticed to visit all these dream artifacts *in situ*.

The same can be said of the vast Versailles royal palace in France. Reportedly Louis XIV used up half the country's financial resources to build it — which of course is unsound — but perhaps, taking into account all the tourists visiting it today, it has "paid off."

One Swedish monarch who gloriously united the role of ruler and patron of the arts was Gustav III. He revitalized Sweden as a nation after a corrupt era, and he favored the arts in many ways. He had a keen interest in theater, performing on stage, and having dinner while still wearing his theatrical costume. However, he soon stopped this habit and ruled with credibility. Unfortunately, he angered elite club forces, and they killed him at the Royal Opera. As a style-conscious king, Gustav died at the theater, suffering a martyr's death as the last Swedish king of note. It is a striking image.

*****

Charles XII was another previous Swedish ruler with a cultural inclination. Josephsson describes some fascinating events. For example, once in Turkey, Charles was inspired by Constantinople's hill of the Sophia mosque and its cypresses. He wanted the Brunkebergsåsen in Stockholm to be similarly adorned. An aquarelle painted by Major Loos is the extant proof of this idea.

Furthermore, the interior of the Hagia Sophia and its Muslim prohibition against images also inspired Charles. This would be the model for a church at Stockholm castle to be built. No catholic opulence, nor statues in the church room for that would be idolatry...! The whole castle, including its exterior, would be in the same style. For example, it would not have any statues on the roof balustrade pedestals and no statue of his father, Charles XI, in the courtyard (as the architect Tessin had proposed). Charles wanted clean shapes and rich materials — gold, bronze, and marble. Simple forms and *the effect of the material:* fine, timeless aesthetics.

The overall style of Charles' kingdom was no-nonsense and straightforward. It was grand and regal — symbolizing *majestas* — but the overall style was comparatively restrained. Official portraits opted for realism, shunning allegory and antique embellishment. Charles' communion silverware was also rather "anti-baroque" and pure in style. And, finally, Charles himself did not wear a wig or an embroidered silk coat as would befit a king. Instead, he was wigless and wore a coarse cloth uniform, which was the ultimate symbol of the Carolian kingdom. Simple but not simplistic; what you see is what you get.

90

*****

Napoleon is another example of a leader with cultural interests. For instance, according to lady-in-waiting Madame de Rémusat, Napoleon received actors and artists at his breakfast table. However, Dumrath doesn't reveal what they spoke about. Therefore, it is a possibility that these receptions were shallow and harmless. Nonetheless, Napoleon is an exemplary image of a ruler maintaining a cultural interest and not only being imbued by reports of statecraft. The cultural element in politics should not be despised. Unfortunately, there were some high-profile authors who were against (or with time turned against) Napoleon, such as Chateaubriand and Madame de Staël.

Dumrath also tells of a meeting between Napoleon and the painter David. At their first meeting, David was at work on a painting, and Napoleon asked him what it was to become.

"Leonidas at Thermopylae, your majesty," David replied.

"You can do better than painting the vanquished," Napoleon said. So David took the hint and painted Napoleon on a white stallion, going up St. Bernhard for his rendezvous with glory.

Regarding architecture Napoleon once said: *"Ce qui est grand est toujours beau"* (big is beautiful). This isn't very profound, but at least it had some idea of architecture. Napoleon didn't merely say, "build what you want."

*****

Adolf Hitler was a 19th-century example of a ruler interested in music (but not a musical ruler in the classical sense). In his writing, Alan Bullock does his best to play down the extent of this musical interest by emphasizing Hitler as only being interested in Wagner, Beethoven, Bruckner, and operettas like Strauss's *Die Fledermaus,* Léhar's *The Merry Widow,* and Donizetti's *Daughter of the Regiment.* In this respect, Bullock may be out of his depth. It is obvious that

Hitler was an avid fan of Wagner. He had attended operas such as *Lohengrin* multiple times. According to his friend August Kubizek, seeing *Rienzi* in Linz as a youth affected Hitler deeply, triggering visions of future grandeur. Another favorite was Wagner's opus *Die Meistersinger von Nürnberg*. He also collected original Wagner opera scores and librettos, and he attended many performances in Bayreuth from 1923 onwards. Hitler's music interest was substantial and Bullock, by attempting to redeem music from the negative shadow of Hitler, deliberately obscures this, which is historical writing at its worst.

*****

Hitler had other cultural interests. He, for instance, had a predilection for pictorial art. He could draw and paint. Comparing Hitler to one of his adversaries who also dabbled in painting, Winston Churchill, Churchill was slightly better at painting. His brushwork was freer, while Hitler's paintings had the character of "mere coloring." However, Hitler was not a bad painter though. His work was not so bad as some deem it to be.

Oddly enough, a third leader at the time also painted in his spare time: Dwight D. Eisenhower. But he had his motifs sketched by someone else, so this comes close to being merely "paint by numbers."

*****

Regarding other WWII leaders and their "musical/cultural ability," we can conclude by stating that Joseph Stalin was a fine dancer. Stalin appeared to be quite at home in the ordinary ballroom moves required by international statesmen at state dinners. In an old Swedish magazine article titled "I Danced with Stalin," there is a report from an Allied woman who visited Russia during the 1940s. She informs us that the Russian leader was limber and had a fine sense of rhythm.

VI. A TRIBUTE TO THE LADIES

This chapter is a tribute to the ladies of rigorism. It is an exposé of willful women from antiquity to our current era.

Herodotus springs immediately into mind when it comes to women of antiquity, for his *Historiae* offers some exemplary accounts in this respect. For example, there is Nitocris, queen of Babylon. When she died, she was interred in a coffin, placed over one of the city's gates. The coffin had an inscription claiming that there was money in it to grab for any future ruler of Babylon. Later, when Darius had taken the city, he found out about this, discovered the coffin — but in it, there was just a note with the following words: "If you had not been insatiably greedy and eager to get money by the most despicable means, you would never have opened the tomb of the dead."[49]

Then there was Tomyris, queen of Massagetes, who defended her country against Cyrus' invasion. A truce was made, and Tomyris wanted peace to be the conclusion, but Cyrus refused and continued the invasion. When he was slain in battle, Tomyris cut off his head and put it in a skin full of blood, fulfilling Cyrus' earlier threat that he would have his fill of blood when he was invading her land.[50]

These were tough women. Herodotus also provides us with another example: Artemisia, captain of a galley in the invasion fleet of Xerxes in 480 BCE. She had a respected position in the fleet, and the king often heeded her advice. Nonetheless, she did one nasty thing at Salamis when the tide of battle had turned against

---

49   Herodotus, p. 117.

50   Ibid, p. 127.

the Persians, and Artemisia ended up in a tight corner. To save her ship, she ordered the ramming and sinking of one of their own "blue force" ships, thus giving her ship the appearance of a Greek vessel so that she could slip away during the ensuing commotion.

This chapter is about "women of rigorism, willful women." However, as a side note, we will examine some of the ordinary women of antiquity. One example of the everyday-reality woman in this era was the wife of Phocion, who, despite her husband being the ruler of Athens, ran a simple household and even kneaded the bread herself. But this was in pre-Hellenistic times, and things were simpler back then. Another record of women in antiquity is provided in Proverbs:

> She considers a field and buys it; from her profits she plants a vineyard. She girds herself with strength, and strengthens her arms. She extends her hand to the poor, yes, she reaches out her hands to the needy. She is not afraid of snow for her household, for all her household is clothed with scarlet. She makes tapestry for herself; her clothing is fine linen and purple.[51]

Then there is a woman of a somewhat different nature, Poppaea Sabina as described by Tacitus. She was the second wife of Nero.

> In this woman, there was everything except decency. Her mother, the most beautiful woman of her time, had given her an honorable name and beauty; her wealth corresponded to her noble birth; her conversation was winning, her talent not insignificant. She showed honesty and devoted herself to debauchery. She rarely appeared in public; when she did, it was with a veil over a part of her face so as not to satisfy curious looks or because it suited her. She never spared her reputation...[52]

---

[51]   31:16-17, 20-22.

[52]   *Annals*, Book XII.

A previous chapter stated that Spartan women had great erotic freedom, but they showed independence even in other areas. Herodotus speaks of the Ionian Aristagoras who, as an operator of the Ionian rebellion, is in Greece to recruit support for this. When he is in Sparta, King Cleomenes listens keenly, but when he hears how far it is to the capital of the Persian kingdom against which one rebels — three months' journey — he turns a deaf ear and asks the Ionian to go home. However, the Ionian makes one last attempt to obtain the support of the Spartans and goes to the king with an olive branch in his hand. "Speak," says the king. "Send away the child first," says Aristagoras, referring to the king's nine-year-old daughter, who happens to be standing by her father's side. But she stays, and the Ionian proceeds to offer the king money to gain him as an ally. The bids are getting higher and higher, finally, when it reaches 50 talents, the girl, Gorgo by name, says: "Father, you had better go away, or the stranger will corrupt you."[53]

Cleomenes appreciates the warning, and Aristagoras leaves unsuccessful. Of course, he has better luck in Athens, but that's another story.

*****

In 6th century Constantinople, the Eastern Empire was shaken by a revolt, the Nīka-rebellion, so named because the rebels shouted: "Nīka! Nīka!" (victory), where they went forth in the streets. This word was also shouted at the Hippodrome races. And indeed, it was the supporter teams of the horse race drivers, the blue and the green, which had instigated the rebellion. These *quadriga* races had previously been a place for voicing political opinions in this authoritarian Empire, and now, in 532 CE, it had developed into a full-blown revolt.

Emperor Justinian ordered the rising to be quelled. For this, general Belisarius rounded up tens of thousands of rebels into

---

53   Herodotus, p. 359.

the Hippodrome and then killed them. It's said that the Emperor stood firm beside his wife, Empress Theodora, who, according to Procopius, said this to him during the height of the crisis:

> Once born a man can't escape death. And for a person who has been the Emperor exile is out of the question. I, for one, support the old wisdom that says, that there is no better burial clothes than the imperial purple!

This is a prime example of "willpower in history, shown by women."

Advancing to Europe and the pre-modern era, we find a somewhat similar and pregnant example, in France of 1789 and "the flight to Varennes." After the storming of the Bastille, the revolution became incrementally radicalized, such as attacks on the royal family, which eventually made them virtual prisoners of the government. The king, Louis XVI, was relatively indolent and passive throughout these events while his wife, Queen Marie Antoinette, stepped in to make some decisions. The most spectacular of these was the flight to Varennes in 1791 when she had contacted her old friend and lover, the Swede Axel von Fersen, to arrange for an escape from France to the eastern border where they would be safe among royalists who had fled the revolution earlier.

The escape didn't quite succeed, but it provides an example of how a queen stepped up and offered resistance in a time of crisis. The same pattern can be seen in the Prussian kingdom of 1806. By then, Napoleon had beaten them in the battles of Jena and Auerstädt — and, in the following process, Queen Louise of Prussia escaped east to continue the resistance. Finally, realizing it was meaningless, she later returned to Prussia to plead for Prussia's cause to Napoleon. This is how Louise became a symbol of German nationalism (while her husband, King Frederick William, had a more passive nature). For instance, in the 1920s, conservative German women founded the Queen Louise League, *Königin-Luise-Bund,* a pro-monarchic women's organization.

Louis Napoleon's wife, Eugénie, is also worth mentioning. During the Franco-Prussian war, when the Emperor was ill, she stepped in to become the "let's fight on" voice for the government. Again, this is willpower in history, executed by a woman.

However, these three women (Marie Antoinette, Louise, Eugénie) merely stepped into power vacuums, made possible by the passivity of their husbands. In this respect, a better Western world female figure is needed, one who consciously, over her whole career, shaped her country with willpower and vision. The obvious example is Margret Thatcher, the prime minister of Britain from 1979-1990.

A book title even springs to mind: *Not a Man to Match Her – Thatcher*. During the British depression on all fronts (economic, political, military), she changed the course of destiny and led the land towards greener pastures. Most importantly, in the Falklands War, she became a successful war leader, virtually a latter-day Churchill.

Mrs. Thatcher is an archetypal example of a female exerting her willpower upon history.

VII. SPENGLERIAN DELIBERATIONS

1. Constituent Parts

From a cultural, historical, and geostrategic point of view, this chapter needs to examine Eurasia to clarify misunderstandings, both historical and temporary.

First, what is Eurasia? What parts make up the whole?

There are, indeed, several parts. Primarily, there is Europe.

Europe is a distinct historical component. Just consider elements such as the *Pope, Habsburg, Napoleon,* and *the EU.* They have all ruled Europe. However, the roots go back further than that. With all its colorful Asian colonies (Asia Minor, the Levant, Egypt), the ancient Roman Empire still had its center of gravity in Europe. Europe was the geopolitical heartland. All the key Emperors were of European origin. The possessions in the Middle East were a periphery of some economic importance, but not of dire geopolitical importance; in that matter, Asia was at best a kind of buffer zone.

From antiquity to the Middle Ages, and even today, Europe is a geopolitical-cultural reality, an indelible niche of historical space-time, one of several building blocks in a "global" puzzle. While "Europe" wasn't a unified political regime during antiquity, it functioned as one, both culturally and geographically, if not *geopolitically.* The very name "Europe" is from Greek mythology. *Europa* was the daughter of Phoenician royalty, who was abducted by Zeus and taken to Crete. Later, *Europa* became a name for the

Greek mainland and, c. 500 BCE, also a term for lands north of Greece. The demarcation line to Asia, even then, was the Bosporus.

*****

Concerning Eurasia, we just ask, what niches or cultures have evolved there through history?

For its part, 'Asia' is too vague as a concept. Instead, for the wise man, the scholar, the student of history, Asia consists of three distinct niches, geographically and historically: the Middle East, India, and China.

The Middle East also includes North Africa: middle eastern rulers have often unfurled their tentacles into this region, transforming the concept of "MENA" — constituted by the Middle East and North Africa — into a viable concept, both historical and contemporary.

Together, Europe, the Middle East, India, and China collectively embody Eurasia. And, by looking at the rest of the world, there are also niches/building blocks/cultures such as Sub-Saharan Africa, North America, and South America, plus peripheral regions such as Australia and the South Pole.

However, the four zones of Eurasia are the historical subjects, forming demarcated cultures throughout history.

2. Roots

Primarily, the roots of Europe begin in antiquity. Rome's *nation-building* took place in Europe; the captured eastern provinces had already matured as states within the Persian kingdom and were soon retaken to be subsumed under the Caliphate. Europe's development — aside from the Roman Empire — can also be found in the Empires of Charles the Great, Habsburg, Napoleon, and the EU. To the east, there is also Russia that clearly belongs with Europe.

Regarding the Middle East, its formation can be traced through the Assyrian Empire, the Persian Empire, the Caliphate, and the Ottoman Empire.

Similarly, the development of India can be seen via the history of Ashoka, Muhammad bin Tughluq (the 1300s), and the Mogul Emperors such as Shah Jahan, Jahangir, and Akbar the Great. Then came the English colonial Empire — *the Raj*. And today, we have the state of Bhārat as a full-fledged heir to the great Empires of India.

Finally, China's historical roots extend back to Shi Huang Di and the Han Empire from the time of the birth of Christ. A stable continuity followed this through dynasties like Tang, Mongols, Ming, and Manchu. Contemporary Communist China has inherited all of this prestigious ancestry.

As for South-East Asia, the western part is influenced by India and the eastern part by China. In other words, South-East Asia is not a separate historic-political niche.

3. "World Conquerors" Who Didn't Conquer the World

There are four different Eurasian cultures: Europe, the Middle East, India, and China. How distinct these building blocks are, is evident when you look at the so-called *world conquerors* — including Djinghis Khan and Alexander. While they may be illustrious conquerors, they never ruled over the whole world or even the whole of Eurasia; they primarily ruled over *one* of its specific cultures. And as far as they made inroads into one or more additional ones, they still had the center of gravity in another.

The enduring Mongolian conquest was China. In all their other gains (India, Central Asia, and Eastern Europe), the Mongols failed to create a lasting impression. However, while no enduring state was built there, the Mongol dynasty in China did have staying power. As for Alexander, he conquered the "world" only in the limited, Greek-ancient meaning: the world known by the Greeks was the

Mediterranean, Greece, Egypt, and the Middle East (plus India). Alexander certainly captured large amounts of these territories, but he did not take China. Indeed, he didn't even know China existed.

Alexander undoubtedly deserves the epithet "the Great," but he was not a "world conqueror." The inroads he made into India were relatively marginal, and he only ruled over a fraction of Europe (Greece).

4. Religious Definition

Thus, Eurasia is characterized by specific niches: geographically and historically, they are the realms in which states exist, and culture is developing and thriving. In Spengler's sense, they are *world cultures:* India, China, the Middle East, and Europe. You can look at religion and see how it defined the cultures in question. Of course, this becomes circular reasoning: the niches are there, and certain religions become predominant in them. However, looking at their main beliefs can clarify what these niches are. The niches/cultures/ major realms (India, China, etc.) become the forms into which the spiritual substance is cast and appears as a space-time *Gestalt*.

What religion, then, dominates the respective realm? In Europe, it's Christianity. In the Middle East, Islam. In India, Hinduism. In China, it's Buddhism. For its part, Taoism and Confucianism in China are subordinate in that they lack answers to the ultimate question, where you go when you die. Buddha provides that answer, not Lao Tse and Confucius.

The existence of religious minorities here and there proves nothing. The dominant religion offers the criteria for this classification.

5. *That's How It Is*

Certainly, there is increased international cooperation today, particularly concerning economic and communicative integration, and there is also *interdependence*. However, for that matter, it is not feasible to erase the specificity and tradition implicit in these cultures.

Religions, traditional culture, and geography still have enormous relevance. The Powers That Be might want us all to identify as consumers, chained to the TV, and moronically accepting every dictum, as lobotomized examples of "*das Man*," willingly led like sheep. However, thankfully, there is some inertia immanent in the system. The Chinese still perform Taoism, the Hindus still praise the gods of their ancestors, Muslims in the Middle East pray to God, and European Christians still gladly sing, "We are going to meet the King." This provides a bedrock for tradition that cannot easily be ground down.

If the world is to be integrated more than today, if globalization should continue, it should be done to conserve the particular nature of each culture.

*****

This pattern of cultures isn't original in the conceptual sense. *Mutatis mutandum,* other history philosophers have used it, such as Arnold Toynbee in *A Study of History* and Oswald Spengler in *The Decline of the West.*

There are some viable aspects in Spengler's opus. Not only is Spengler's book highly readable, it also has other fine qualities.

Like Toynbee, Spengler has a perspective that embraces "separate cultures," which could be seen to counter the mainstream attitude revolving around the "development of civilization," where everything is thought to have been on an unstoppable path to glory since the dawn of time in Mesopotamia 4,000 BCE, encompassing both individuals and cultures. However, this concept of separate cultures offers a more diversified image of history than mere progress towards glorious globalization.

Further, Spengler speaks of civilization's growth, blossoming, and decay. Some traits are acquired from one culture to the next. For example, the West has its roots in Rome and Greece's Mediterranean antiquity, but Spengler denied this. However, the very statement *"cultures developing through a pattern à la in the beginning being strong and simple, then adult and realist and finally old and decadent,"* is needed today when no influential scholar at all even hints at the possibility that cultures might decline and collapse.

Egypt is a prime example of this. An Old Kingdom diorite statue of King Khafre is utterly different from a New Kingdom statue of a fat official, and decadence is likely the reason for this discrepancy. Another example occurs with Greek statues: they are strong and clear-cut in pre-Hellenic times but weak and emotionalist in Hellenic times. Now, each period may have its advantages, for fine art was made in all of them — but — to get some clarity when looking at world history, the basic developing pattern of "simple, realist, and decadent" has to be acknowledged.

Spengler's ideas on the lifecycles of cultures with birth, blossom, and death are relevant to our age. However, Spengler's work is no mere *Untergangsromantik*, no simple indulgence in dark forebodings, although there might be a risk of interpreting him that way. It's said that radical conservatives have a tendency to dwell on pessimistic subjects, to secretly rejoice in the death and destruction of a society gone wrong, and maybe Spengler's book caters to that urge somehow.

However, with the help of Spengler, we can face the transformation of civilizations. This outlook requires sobriety to understand ourselves and the world. In our culture, in the current *international world-city civilization,* we are now in a phase of confusion. This leads to reruns, recycling, parodies, and copies. No one takes anything seriously anymore. All that remains is consumerism, populism, and *panem et circensis*. Nietzsche's "Last Man" rules supreme.

We seem to be at the end of a great era. Spengler says that our culture, the West, the Faustian confluence, stood at its height around 1600-1700. Since then, we've mostly seen degeneration, the repetition of styles, and dilettantism. The artists of the good old days — Bach, Rafael, Milton — created works with good measure (Greek *mêtron*), learning their craft and confidently producing work after work. The artists of the later romantic era had to go beyond that and couldn't just repeat the greatness of older works. But in order to do so, they had a tendency to attempt to reach the unreachable, and often failed in the task. For instance, there is Ezra Pound's outcry about his *Cantos* cycle: "I can't make it cohere!" That never happened to the masters of the great era.

This is a clever observation by Spengler. He believes it to be exemplified by Wagner. Sometimes, such as the latter stages of *The Ring*, Wagner can't really make it cohere. Wagner was great, but occasionally the crevices and paddings are nevertheless apparent in his Great Work. It's somewhat devoid of measure — *mêtron*.

6. Western Triumph

Spengler is correct in his critique of late-period Faustian culture. However, he shouldn't be read too programmatically. For example, if everything in the West after 1700 is *Entartung* and degeneration, then, consequently, Spengler's work, *The Decline of the West* (1918-1922), can't be taken seriously. Therefore, one should not focus solely on the element of decline. Spengler himself privately admitted that after the publication of his work and Europe and the West gathered strength following WWI, the book's title should have been "*The Triumph of the West*." For, implicitly through all the analyses of his work, his constructs from which the pattern of rise-blossoming-decay are to be proven runs a great *admiration* of the West and its culture, even after the supposed apex of the 17th century. It's the Faustian culture, symbolized by Goethe's Faust, who wants to do everything, know everything, experience everything. Spengler exudes veritable praise for the Faustian world, for its geniuses in their cells probing the depths of existence, for its explorers mapping every blank patch of the globe, for its inventors inventing previously unseen things, and for its schoolboys drawing dream cars in the hope of driving them along never-ending highways: *"I'm heading out to the highway... Roll on down the highway... Midnight on a never-ending highway..."*

The West is akin to an architecture where the front necessarily must *express* something. This is a typical western trait, which is not always immediately perceptible. Yet, as Spengler holds, Christian temples speak loudly about their interior, Muslim temples remain silent about it, and the temples of antiquity don't even think about it. Spengler concludes that the cathedral starts from within, the ancient temple from without, and the mosque both begins and ends in its interior, in its gilded, arabesque-fretted grotto. Few other scholars can write such succinct and symbolically telling summaries.

7. Goethe and Nietzsche

The West is about central perspective and analytical languages, about a marching, drum-induced pace along boulevards that seemingly lose themselves in the hazy distance à la Champs Elysées, Unter den Linden, Valhallavägen, and Sunset Boulevard. The symbol of the West is the *plain,* and that of the Middle East is the *cave.*

In Spengler's vein, the West is about the city, the Faustian city with its fountains, squares, parks, and boulevards. It has unique elements in a unique creation, living with it and dying with it. But as long as it lives, we can walk in these megacities and feel sentimental about the beauty of these fronts with their *cranea,* volutes, and gargoyles, and these interiors with their galleries, exedras, cupolas, and pilasters, and the halls and marble tables with gold inscriptions like these:

> If in Infinity the Self forever flows
> repeated endlessly in endless repetition
> so arch the sure and numberless porticoes
> upon themselves with force and impartition;
> from everything out-surges love for life,
> from vastest star to smallest kernel
> and every pressure, agony and strife
> is in the Lord our God but rest eternal.

This poem by Goethe (*"Wenn im unendlichen"*) was a *Leitmotif* for Spengler's work: it was the cyclical, recurring pattern in the development of cultures that he wanted to capture. There are other Goethean influences — Faust, of course (when Spengler names our culture "Faustian"), and the tendency to see a human culture etc., as an *organism* and not a *mechanism*. Other than that, Spengler was influenced by Nietzsche, and here primarily by his Dionysian thought, his vision of the archaic, pre-classic antiquity. The archaic Greek era had a dreamlike quality, where rural people lived in trance-like states bringing intuition to the fore, in contrast to the later urban times where sobriety, transparency, and analysis came to dominate. Spengler saw the same pattern repeat itself in early European times with the Edda being sung in misty German forests, exuding a dream-saturated, adolescent power that slowly matured in the city culture (civilization) and became overripe in the world city, in the phase we now live in: *international world-city civilization.*

8. Urban Fatigue

Eulogies for the West aside, we now live in more-or-less decadent times: the signs are obvious; just read the writing on the wall. However, after reading papers and watching TV, it is clear that today's pundits don't see these signs. Instead, they believe in a never-ending liberal utopia just around the corner, only becoming real if we enhance specific aspects such as education, communication, or commerce in a quantitative fashion. Therefore, a Spenglerian analysis comes in handy here. Why exactly are we running out of steam? Why is our current culture lacking vigor...?

As intimated, the Faustian culture emerged in medieval days and blossomed around 1600-1700. Barring some good works of art after this in general, it's a dismal time, a time of decadence. One of these is the cult of the *novel*, which defines a long prose narrative as the optimal expression of literature. Gone is the archaic, noble *héroïde* sung in metric stanzas; instead, there are bourgeois classics, urban narratives about shopkeepers, dandies, criminals, and demimondes. Spengler held that the latter-day epics focus on the doings of a Nana, a Bel-Ami, or a Hertha, and they're all sterile. The modern novel is a product of the city and has nothing significant to offer mankind in the future, not to future men who will live in a more authentic culture. It might be using Guillaume Faye's concept, to become an *archeofuturist* world.

However, Spengler is not an infallible prophet in every regard. The future for the West is not fixed in stone. For example, Rudolf Steiner believed in more extended periods of cultures. Steiner thought that the Antique, Graeco-Roman culture started in 747 BCE and ended as late as 1413 CE, giving it a length of 2,160 years. In the same "astrological era" periodicity (applied by Steiner to all cultures after the fall of Atlantis), our Faustian culture took up the fallen mantle of the Graeco-Roman culture in 1413 and is set to last until 3573.

The exactitude of the dates may appear astounding, but there are indicia of them being watershed years. For example, 1413 was when Jeanne d'Arc appeared, providing a spiritual beacon for European renewal. A few years later, she liberated her land from foreign occupation. In other parts of Europe, more nationalists followed, like Hus and Engelbrekt. There was also a cultural explosion in Italy ("the Renaissance"), and European sea-farers set forth to discover the world. This was a new era — the Faustian era.

This Faustian culture will — as perceived by Steiner — only end in 3573. This gives us plenty of time to remedy the decadence.

In comparison, Spengler had a narrow outlook. The lifespan of his cultures — 1,000-1,500 years — is too short. Conversely, the Steiner pattern (2,160 years) gives us more room to maneuver.

Spengler is also a born pessimist. In *Man and Technics,* Spengler writes that "optimism is cowardice." Future for mankind is merely a fight to the death against nature, and then *finis.* This is where Spengler fails. To balance his negative outlook, perspectives like those of Steiner are required. Humanity requires a cosmic pattern that provides room for continued striving and continued existence for man — especially for Faustian man.

9. The City

The civilization of today is that of an international world city culture. An elite, traveling from mega city to mega city, governs us, yet they feel lost in the nearest countryside. Spengler stated this in the chapter "The Soul of the City" of his magnum opus, and it's still viable. The Faustian city originates as an extended village, grows in medieval times around a castle or a dome, blossoms in early modern times, and progressively declines forever after. The decline, not apparent on the surface — which shines more than ever — but since nothing new is created, everything is just a repetition of styles, nostalgia, and romanticism.

The fact that the current era provides nothing but repetition and recycling, pastiche, parody, and remakes is apparent to everyone. Everything basks in the glory of past masters, making covers and commentaries, which only mimic the originality of actual creators. The demand for "originality" is long gone — the words *cultural fatigue* spring immediately into mind.

Spengler points these details out to us, even though he sometimes makes broad generalizations and is too pessimistic. Everything is not lost. Individuals, the "aristocrats of the soul," can survive the decay by their erudition and willpower to become the leaders of a new era, stretching to the 3500s.

VIII. THE ROLE OF TEMPLES

It's been said that the temple is "a bridgehead for the divine." It's a place to meet God, to have sermons, perform rituals, and is a place of meditation. A temple (used here as a synonym for 'church') is also a node of the landscape and the cityscape, a symbol of culture and human striving, and not just an institution of any particular religious sect. There is a formal, ceremonial role present, but the temple also has a significant aesthetic and emotional role, both exterior and interior.

Consider the exterior of temples and the symbolic role of the building as an element of any landscape. This role is crucial — for a landscape without churches, or a city without temples is devoid of soul. Spengler says that for a city to be called a city, to be felt and experienced as a city, it has to have a soul ("The Soul of the City" in *The Decline of the West*, 1922). An old, small town with rich and variegated architecture may have more of a 'city feeling' than a newly built city of millions. Nor is the prevalence of temples unimportant to impart soul to a city. Any city worthy of its name must have temples at crucial nodes. They are as important as parks and squares. Conversely, a city with only apartment blocks, offices, and malls, is destined to become titanic and sterile.

How should a temple look? Is there an ideal style? Indeed, it is safe to say that there are no ugly temples...! Temples are like LP album covers, which my brother used to say are never ugly; the very format of a 30 x 30 cm square cover is ideal for any artwork, the ideal ice rink on which to graphically skate.

As for the form of churches, there may be traditional rules of thumb, such as an altar in the eastern part, towards the sunrise. Other than that, an architect is free to have towers in the east or the west, large or small windows, and an interior in either light or subdued colors. As such, a church is both a challenge and a green pasture for an architect. The rules are scarce, like poetry.

In Lutheran churches, the interior was mainly whitewashed, and this color has a role in northern churches. However, when building churches of brick (as northerners are wont to do), a warm feeling emerges when the interior avoids whitewash and instead opts for naked dark red brick. For instance, Stockholm's neo-gothic St. Johannes church has a warm, inviting interior with red brick walls. Conversely, as was the case after the Reformation, the whitewash gothic dome interiors can be seen as Puritanism gone astray in a wilderness of nihilism.

What is the role of a church? Along with sermons and services, it's to be there as a place of meditation and private devotion. It always has been and always shall be. Today, this is a way to give individualism a role within the church at large, without castigating individuals as antisocial. This author, once in Stockholm, was killing time between arrivals and departures. Being in the Old Town, he went to the Stockholm dome, a medieval church with a classical exterior and a reasonably warm, gothic interior with brick pillars. This was in the summer with abundant tourists and an entry fee. There was also a sign which announced, "For private meditation, no fee." How generous and spiritual.

However, tourists do have a role to play. Places like Notre Dame de Paris, the dome of Cologne, and even the Uppsala dome have a lot of visitors each year. This is indicative of spiritual instinct, even though it can also become 'industrial' (you "have to" see the dome, hastily take your photos, then leave). Temples deserve reverence from both the visitors and the church authorities. For example, to sell souvenirs inside the temple itself is close to blasphemy. "The house of my Father shall be a house of prayer, and you made it into a den of thieves..."

A temple is not primarily a museum, nor merely a tourist attraction. People may go there to appreciate its aesthetics, but primarily it's a house of prayer, a place of meditation, and a bridge to the divine. So strolling around eating ice cream and absent-mindedly looking at 'stuff' should be done for the main street. When *in ecclesiam*, strive to be ecclesiastical.

When on sacred ground, let's allow sacredness to invade our being.

IX. AVIATOR AUTHORS

The best example of a pilot who is also an author is Antoine de Saint-Exupéry (1900-1944). He pioneered the role and defined it. With a spiritual elevation in his texts, he became something of a saint, a real-life angel descending from heaven to bring a message of peace and joy to the world. However, he wasn't merely a philosopher behind the stick. He was also a combat pilot in WWII. Prior to that, he flew the postal route to colonial North Africa, which was no picnic. It took willpower, to say the least. So, Saint-Ex and other aviator authors (Roald Dahl, Joseph Heller, Jim Ballard, Åke Hodell), are the subjects of this chapter. They were eternal symbols of willpower and vision in the 20th century.

1. The End of Saint-Ex

It was 8.30 in the morning on 31 July 1944. A Lockheed P-38 Lightning, unarmed recce version, took off from the Burgo field on northern Corsica. The pilot was Major Antoine de Saint-Exupéry of the Free French forces.

His mission was to reconnoiter from the Riviera over Grenoble to the Annecy region. This was in the run-up to the Allied invasion of Southern France in the middle of August, Operation Anvil. The pictures Saint-Ex would take with his aircraft would be part of the reconnaissance before the attack.

The P-38 had fuel for six hours. By 2.30 pm, the group was pessimistic about his chances of returning. His aircraft was never found, and after three months, Saint-Ex was declared as Missing in Action.

Later a German admirer of Saint-Ex, one Hermann Korth, read an article of this fateful last flight. Korth had been in the Luftwaffe during the war, and he had papers saying that an enemy aircraft had been seen going down in flames on the afternoon of 31 July 1944, not far from the Corsican coast. The time and place were in accordance with data held by the Free French air corps; this was noted by Saint-Ex's publisher when he took part of Korth's information. Later it was proposed that it was two Focke-Wulf 190s from a unit based in Avignon that had been sent to intercept the aircraft of Saint-Ex and shoot him down.

This information was made available in the 1990s. It is not possible now to identify the German pilot or pilots who shot him down. However, details aside, it may not be so easy to step forward and say that you're the man who killed the author of *The Little Prince*.

2. Airmail Pilot

Saint-Ex (a signature he used) graduated as a French air force officer in 1922. This information is in Webster's biography. However, there was little to do in the peacetime service, so Saint-Ex soon left and tried diverse civilian careers. Nevertheless, his real aviator's life began in 1926 when he took a job with the airline Latécoère.

Pierre-George Latécoère began shipping post by air to Spain and Northern Africa after WWI. In 1925 a regular line was established between Toulouse and Dakar. Saint-Ex and other pilots flew aircraft of the type Breguet 14, double-deckers with open cockpits. This is vividly described in the Saint-Ex novel *Courrier Sud*. In 1928 the aircraft were replaced with Latécoère 28s, high-winged monoplanes with closed cockpits and radio. It became safer then but somewhat less pioneering and elemental than the open-cockpit, double-decker days.

Having flown the route Toulouse-Casablanca, Saint-Ex was transferred to the desert route between Cape Juby in Spanish Sahara to Dakar in Senegal. Due to recurrent mechanical failures, the aircraft flew in pairs. If the post plane had to go down, the escort plane also landed, took over the mailbags, and flew on. The post must always get through; it was a case of upholding the communications with the colonial empire. Communications are vital to any community. In this heroic life, Saint-Ex thrived, and his novel *Courrier Sud* (English version, *Southern Mail*) testifies it. It embodies the challenge of the elements, the danger, and a man's life. Conversely, before this career, he had worked as a traveling salesman of trucks. During the entire year, he sold only one.

Accidents were common in the aerial service. There were also hostile Arab tribes on the ground, and the Western Sahara had only recently been pacified.

3. Record Attempts

Southern Mail came out in 1929, and more books followed, so Saint-Ex was becoming known as the airman author. During the 1930s, with the exceptions of journalism and book writing, Saint-Ex made record attempts, which ended fatefully. The last was in Guatemala in February 1938. When taking off from Guatemala City in a Caudron Simon, the plane was too heavy and didn't take to the air properly. As a result, it crashed, and Saint-Ex was hospitalized for weeks. The heaviness might have been because Saint-Ex had given the amount of fuel to be filled in liters, which his aide had interpreted as gallons. One gallon is equivalent to 3.8 liters.

The record attempt in question concerned pioneering the 14,000 km route New York-Patagonia, backed by the French ministry of air.

The first record attempt by Saint-Ex was in 1935, which was more interesting. Events such as this became the basis for the majority of Saint-Ex writings, both fiction and essays. It was the encounter with the desert as a psychological landscape, a landscape of myth and moral. Q.v. *The Little Prince, Wind, Sand and Stars, Citadelle.*

Saint-Ex and his aide would fly the route Paris-Saigon in less than 99 hours to win a prize of 150,000 francs. The plane was a Caudron 630 Simon, a fast, low-winged plane, cream-colored with red stripes. On the leg of Benghazi-Cairo, the wind imperceptibly changed from tailwind to headwind. It was cloudy, and Saint-Ex lost his orientation. He went down to scout and then hit the ground. The plane slid a bit on a stretch of smooth pebbles but still had relatively high speed and eventually crashed.

The two airmen were unhurt but stranded in the desert. After finishing their meager food and water rations, they stayed by the wreck for days, as was the custom then. But eventually, they decided to venture out and headed east. They saw mirages and were about to succumb to thirst. Finally, they saw a Bedouin on a hill. They approached him and he gave them all the care they required.

The flight was a failure, but when returning to France, Saint-Ex was still hailed as a national hero.

4. WWII

When WWII broke out in September 1939, Saint-Ex was called up into the air force. He was stationed east of Paris with the reconnaissance group 2/33 and promoted to captain. To begin with, they flew the comparatively slow Potez 63, which was soon replaced by the faster Bloch 174. Both these designs were two-engine, double-fin type aircraft with radial engines.

Winter and spring passed by without notable action in the *Phoney War* reality, with the French and British waiting for the Germans to attack. The attack came on 10 May 1940. The Germans had amassed their armor for a thrust through the weakly defended Ardennes. The frontline was soon broken through, and the panzer columns advanced steadily westward onto the English Channel coast. The 2/33 group took part in the defense. For example, on the 23rd of May Saint-Ex and his crew were ordered to scout towards Arras. Saint-Ex speaks of this in *Pilot de Guerre (Flight to Arras)*.

On that sunny day of spring, the Bloch 174 took off with Saint-Ex at the controls, escorted by three Devoitine fighters. Hundreds of enemy tanks were seen near Arras. German flak ensued, but Saint-Ex turned to take cover in a cloud. Six Me 109s engaged the escort fighters. Two Devoitines were shot down — but — Saint-Ex's friend, Jean Schneider, flying the third, kept defending himself until his aircraft was hit and he had to bail out. Only lightly injured, when he returned to the French lines, he believed he had failed to protect Saint-Ex. He, for one, was also dejected, believing that Schneider had died while defending him. Nevertheless, when the two men were later reunited at the hospital where Schneider was resting, they were both merry.

Group 2/33 maintained photo surveillance of the German advance, although the battle was already lost. As the British evacuated via Dunkirk and the French government entered an armistice with Hitler, 2/33, for its part, successively regrouped to North Africa but then had to surrender. During this phase, Saint-Ex and a colleague were ordered to fetch four new Bloch 174s from a field near Bordeaux, and, finally there, they were met by the sight of hundreds of combat aircraft, grouped wingtip by wingtip. So whatever France was lacking in 1940, it certainly wasn't spare aircraft.

5. Exile and Return

After the surrender, Saint-Ex stayed in France for a while. However, when the opportunity arrived to go to the US and continue the fight from there, he went.

In the US, Saint-Ex wrote *Flight to Arras* and *The Little Prince*. Then there was an Allied drive to invade Europe, seeking a feasible entry-level by landing in North Africa. They did this. By May 1943, the British and Americans had forced the Axis to surrender in Tunis, and at about the same time, Saint-Ex arrived with American reinforcements. He was again subsumed into his old unit, 2/33, now having transferred its loyalty to the Free French. The unit was equipped with American Lockheed P-38 Lightnings.

The unit was based in Tunis in Tunisia. Saint-Ex flew his first mission in July 1943, scouting over southern France. Unfortunately, on the next mission, he engaged the wheel breaks too late after landing and crashed, leading to his suspension from flying. Some months on the ground would follow, but thanks to friends in high places, he could soon fly again, having been given the right to fly five missions. This quota was quickly exceeded.

It was now the spring of 1944, and the group was based in Corsica. After Saint-Ex's arrival on the scene, the time had seen an Allied landing on Sicily (July 1943) and then the Italian landings (August). The advance through Italy was slow, and it only reached Rome in July 1944. At the same time, there was the planning of the southern French landings (cooperating with the Normandy D-Day landings of June 1944), and Saint-Ex was shot down during a scout for this.

6. The Author

Three distinct classical books by Saint-Ex are *Southern Mail, Wind, Sand and Stars,* and *The Little Prince.*

Southern Mail isn't just about the heroic feats of a double-decker pilot on the desert postal route. It's about his whole life, shown in flashbacks. The book is in the charming format of the French master, *the short novel,* and is about 100 pages in length.

Wind, Sand, and Stars accurately render Saint-Ex's life as a pilot. It features anecdotes, poetic descriptions of nature as seen from the cockpit, and moral lessons, all of much are incomparable.

Finally, *The Little Prince* has a naïve charm. Children may read it, but on the whole, it's more than a children's book. It is an existential story told in simple — but not simplistic — terms. The most profound wisdom in the book is this: looking at the sky and not seeing a particular planet, you still know it's there. This is the coda of esotericism, the reality of the invisible strain of existence.

7. Roald Dahl

Roald Dahl (1916-1990) is primarily known as an author. His days as an RAF fighter pilot are less known, although they were published in his memoir *Going Solo*. This book is a modest memoir: Dahl plays down the heroic role he played as a fighter pilot in Greece 1941. However, he did possess heroism. One cannot lightheartedly enter a dogfight with Me 109s and live to tell the tale. As a fighter pilot, Dahl was, on the whole, a credible figure.

Let's begin *in medias res,* in the middle of the action. During April 1941, on an Egyptian RAF airfield, the Squadron Leader called on Pilot Officer Dahl and said:

> "See that Hurricane over there?"
> "Indeed," Dahl said, "what about it?"
> "Take it and fly to Greece."
> "What? But I'm not trained on the Hurricane!"
> "Nonsense. Away with you!"

In other words, Dahl had to muster his will to get going and take off. Unfortunately, he was slightly too tall for a fighter pilot and had to sit bent in the cockpit. By the time he reached Crete he had cramps in his legs. After 4 ½ hours, he landed on an RAF base outside Athens: Eleusis. He had to be carried from the plane.

As for Greece, it was first attacked by Italy in the spring of 1940, and the English soon decided to intervene and defend it, in the spring of 1941 having 60,000 men and 200 aircraft on the scene.

They were needed, for the Germans had taken over the stalled Greek campaign from their Italian allies by April.

Dahl arrived in Greece as one of the last reserves. The fighting was fierce, and the British were performing a fighting retreat, airwise opposing more than 800 German aircraft. It was the heroics of the Battle of Britain again, the main difference being that this theatre of war was a mere sideshow to the British public.

8. Ju 88

Dahl had joined the RAF in 1939, and this was one of his first actual combat missions. 80 Squadron to which he belonged had the task of fighting Germans bombing ships outside Chalcis, the chief town of the island Euboea. For the Hurricanes, the tactics were to fight one by one, not supporting each other in combat pairs as was the usual custom. It was perilous, even more so for Dahl due to his lack of experience.

After some time flying, Dahl eventually reached Chalcis. Then German bombers appeared, Junkers Ju 88s, flying in line and Dahl approaching them from above. The formation flew into a mountainous area, flying close together and following a valley whereby only the last plane could fire at Dahl. For his part, Dahl aimed at one of the engines of this Ju 88 and fired. The salvo hit, and the plane went down. The crew bailed out.

Dahl returned to base and reported. Later he was to hear that you should never hang on to the tail of a Ju 88.

*****

The missions continued as the Germans advanced. Soon only onetenth remained of the 200 British planes. The 80 Squadron was also decimated. Dahl, however, shot down another Ju 88 during a mission, following which enemy bombers began to be escorted by Messerschmitt 109s.

The RAF pilots were constantly busy, sometimes doing four sorties per day. On the 20th of April, the Battle of Athens occurred. The Squadron sent all twelve Hurricanes. At 2,500 meters' altitude over Athens, the enemy attacked them — more than 200 Me 109s and 110s. In his memoir, *Going Solo*, Dahl tells us how the sky was a blur of enemy planes coming towards him. However, he kept his cool, continued maneuvering, and each time he had a German in his sight, he fired. At one point, Dahl saw a man whose Hurricane was on fire step out onto the wing and jump. Dahl kept fighting until he was out of ammo. He didn't know if he had shot down anyone, and there wasn't time to check on the results. The sky was so full of aircraft that he had to avoid collisions half the time.

It was truly an epic air battle.

When Dahl returned to base, his rudder was damaged, but he could maneuver passably with his ailerons. Five of the Squadron's planes had been shot down. On the same day, the base was also attacked by Me 109s, forcing Dahl to fly more missions during the afternoon.

The next day the Squadron was relocated to a field close to the coast. The planes were left there to be flown by more experienced pilots to Egypt. The pilots of the 80 Squadron were to be evacuated in a DeHavilland Rapide, a short-haul airliner mainly made of plywood. The Battle of Greece was over, and the Germans had won.

9. Flight Career

In 1939 Dahl was in Tanzania, East Africa, part of the British Empire, as a Shell official. In November, he joined the Royal Air Force, which had a base in nearby Nairobi, Kenya. For training, they flew Tiger Moths, a charming double-decker with room for a teacher and a student. Then, when he had reached the level of solo flyer, Dahl enjoyed performing this trick with the Tiger Moth: When rolling over and flying upside down, the engine stopped. Rolling back restarted the engine. In the former position, the carburetor didn't get any petrol.

Dahl loved the training. He was young, the petrol was free, and the sights were splendid from the cockpit: Kenya with its savannahs, mountains, and wildlife. He had the habit of flying low over buffalo hoards who panicked when he swept over them.

In September 1940, Dahl was stationed in Western Egypt, now having won his wings, and became an officer of the RAF. During this time, Italy attacked Egypt from its base in Libya. One day Dahl was ordered to rebase a Gloster Gladiator. He got lost, crashed, and was hospitalized with head injuries. Dahl was given the option to be sent home but refused since this would have meant an end to flying.

After the Greek intermezzo, 80 Squadron was grouped in Palestine. Their mission was to attack Vichy French airfields in Syria. The Middle East was turning German-friendly, and therefore the British had decided to maintain a military presence.

Further air battles ensued. The Germans, based in Greece, could easily reach the Levant. However, for Dahl, his flight career was nearly over. He was suffering from blackouts and headaches, *sequelae* of the Gladiator crash. Dahl was sent home on medical grounds. He sent a telegram to his mother and sisters in England.

"Will soon arrive by boat. Syrian War fun. Tell me if you need anything."

He didn't get a reply, but he nevertheless soon came home, bringing a bag of oranges as a gift.

After taking leave, Dahl was up for his next assignment as an air attaché in Washington, a post he held for the remainder of the war.

10. Literary Career

During his American stay, Dahl began writing. His literary debut was a short story dramatizing the Gladiator crash: "Shot Down over Libya." A diverse range of texts followed this, and then, in the 60s, he had a breakthrough in the genre of children's books with *James and the Giant Peach*. After this, there was the classic *Charlie and the Chocolate Factory*: a tale of wish fulfillment with vivid imagery to which both children and adults could relate. In addition, it contained modern fairy tale elements, such as *a factory* being the mythical venue and the factory owner himself being a curious mixture of CEO and devil/trickster/tempter.

Dahl's adult horror stories *Tales of the Unexpected* must also be mentioned: restrained and elegant, they left a lot to the reader's imagination. As for his memoirs, apart from *Going Solo,* we have a volume entitled *Boy: Tales of Childhood,* which is a very fascinating and readable account of his early life.

11. Air Attaché

Another exciting episode occurs when Dahl, as an air attaché in Washington during the war, chanced upon some critical documents. The US planned to take over all European air traffic after the war, and an American friend had let Dahl read some government documents on the subject. This occurred one night in the summer of 1943, and Dahl's friend was Charles Marsh, a millionaire and publicist. The author of the documents was US vice president George Wallace. Dahl, realizing the value of the papers, made a copy and returned them. According to Dahl, the papers were later read by Churchill, who had an outbreak of anger.

He had a reason for it. The Americans were planning to let Pan American Airways become world dominant. PanAm had underlined the need for an American civil air hegemony. The whole affair didn't lead to anything (except for some diplomatic protest), but it illustrates American self-confidence at the time. The US believed that the glory days of Europe would end after the war. To some extent, they were correct, but Europe did not become a mere backwater. Both American and European airlines traversed the globe after the war.

12. Diverse

After returning home to England in 1941, Dahl was out walking one night in London. Then some inebriated army soldiers on leave saw him, saying, "There's an officer, get him!" But on closer examination, someone saw his dark blue uniform and said, "No, it's an RAF guy, leave him!" That, in a nutshell, is called possessing a "good reputation." After the Battle of Britain, the RAF had a unique, untouchable aura among the British.

Both Dahl's parents, Sophie and Harald Dahl, came from Norway. Harald had become the co-owner of a ship brokerage in Cardiff, Wales. He died when Roald was about one. This, and the early death of a sister, according to Dahl himself, made him familiar with the *morbid* element of life, which later became a driving force in his writing.

When Dahl was air attaché in Washington, as a part of intelligence gathering, he befriended many American ladies. For instance, he met Claire Boothe Luce, who was married to the owner of *Time* and *Life* magazines. After the third night with Luce, Dahl allegedly said the following to his chief, the British ambassador Lord Halifax:

> "You see, this is a marvelous task, but I just can't go on. I'm totally exhausted."
> The ambassador nodded and said:
> "Roald, did you ever see the Charles Laughton film about Henry VIII?"

"Yes," Dahl said.

"Well," said Halifax, "do you remember the scene where Henry goes into the bedroom with Anne of Cleves, and he turns around and says: 'What haven't I done for England!' That's how you must do."

13. Joseph Heller

This exposé of aviator authors has it all: an angelic reconnaissance pilot (Saint-Ex), a formidable fighter pilot (Dahl), and now a conscientious bombardier: Joseph Heller. He wrote the bestseller *Catch-22*, based on his experiences during WWII as a bombardier, the man in the front of the bomber aiming at the ground and ordering the felling of the bombs.[54]

Heller has told us of his air force career in *A 'Catch-22' Casebook*, an anthology with texts about the novel. Heller arrived on the island of Corsica in May 1944 as a 21-year-old NCO in the US Air Force. He was placed as a bombardier in a B-25 group in Cervione.

The first mission meant bombing a bridge outside of Florence, Italy, in Poggibonsi. The Germans were grouped in this place because the Pope had asked both belligerents to spare nearby Siena, which was the birthplace of Italy's patron saint St. Catherine.

During the mission, Heller's task was to keep his eyes on the plane leading the formation — when it opened its bomb bay, Heller would open his. And when the bombs of the leader plane started to fall, Heller would push the button to release his.

There was no flak over the target. Instead, the leading plane began a long, straight approach. Heller dozed. When he awoke, he saw how the bombs fell from the other aircraft, and he began releasing his own. The others hit the bridge; Heller's bombs hit a mountainside several kilometers away.

---

[54] Disclaimer: this book is about the influence of willpower upon history. However, Heller, like the last figure in this survey, Hodell, isn't a paragon of willpower. Rather the opposite.

Another time they were to bomb a bridge in southern France. The navigator of Heller's plane had been a history teacher before the war, and when they flew over Orange, he said:

> "To the right we see Orange, ancestral home of the kings of Holland and Wilhelm III, who governed England from 1688 through 1702."
>
> "And to the left," a machine gunner interrupted over the intercom, "we have flak."

14. Background

In the summer of 1944, the Allies were in their second year of combat in Italy. The intent was to invade Hitler's "Festung Europa" from an unexpected direction — but — it wasn't so easy; the hilly terrain of the Apennine peninsula favored the defender. It was reminiscent of Korea. As a result, Italy wasn't completely captured until May 1945. The Germans had occupied Italy in the summer of 1943, when the Italians had surrendered to the Allies.

Heller and his comrades in 340 Bomb Group had volunteered for the service; they were well paid and well-fed. After the fall of Rome taking leave became a popular pastime. It was well cared for, and the quartermaster of the Group had rented two posh apartments, one with five rooms for the officers and one with fifteen for the NCOs.

Once during such a Roman leave, Heller and a comrade were walking in the city. Suddenly a young, portly figure approached them and dragged them into his shop, where he drew caricatures of them. He asked them their names, made them pay him, and then threw them out. His name was Federico Fellini, later a famous director with films like *La Dolce Vita* and *8 1/2*.

By this time, the Germans had no aircraft to defend Italy with, only flak (*Fliegerabwehrkanone* — anti-aircraft guns). For their part, the American planes had no fighter escort. However, most of the missions flown by 340 were short, roughly three hours in duration, and relatively safe. Heller's group didn't lose a plane until 3 June 1944. It was only in his 20th mission that Heller saw friendly aircraft being shot down. Heller has said that until then, it had mostly been a game, but now, it became serious.

15. The End

It was on 15 August 1944 that Operation Anvil was about to commence. This was the Allied invasion of southern France, the same one in which Saint-Ex flew his last, lethal mission. The B-25s would bomb the bridge over the River Rhône by the city of Avignon. One mission to this target had already been completed, the one when Heller first saw one of the blue force planes go down. Fortunately, the crew escaped with parachutes.

This was Heller's 37th mission, and he had 23 more to go. Precisely what happened over Avignon during this second mission is unclear. However, we gather from Heller that suddenly the co-pilot took control of the plane. Heller, placed in the nose as the bombardier should be, didn't know this. He saw another plane hit in an engine, lose a wing, and crash. There were no parachutes. Then his plane dropped its bombs. Heller tells us that the plane started diving, and he was nailed to the cabin roof. Some nerve-racking moments followed until it leveled out, after which they flew through flak. Heller's headset was shut off, and this caused some confusion. The pilot thought that Heller was injured — which was the origin of the "help the bombardier" line in *Catch-22*. Heller was unhurt, but the forward machine gunner had an injured leg. Heller assisted him, and the plane made it back to base. The gunner was taken care of, and he recovered. However, Heller was shocked by the whole experience and asked to be grounded, stop going on bombing missions, and serve on the ground instead. This was granted, and soon he was sent home to the States — by boat.

After the war, Heller promised himself never to set foot in a plane again. But after having spent too many hours on the train between Miami and New York, he began to fly again.

16. *Catch-22*

After the war, Heller began a career in advertising while writing the novel *Catch-22*. The book is based on Heller's war experience, even though a lot of it is made up, absurd, and unlikely. The setting revolves around American airmen based on Corsica in 1944, the main character being the bombardier Yossarian who has had enough of flying.

Catch-22 has some value as a satire. The USA, the greatest nation in the world, vanquisher of Nazism, is portrayed as an absurd power and a ruthless war machine. Looking at WWII America and its Air Force, Heller captured the current zeitgeist, that of the 50s and the emerging 60s. *Catch-22* soon became a bestseller and was made into a film in 1970. The book is better than the film; the film suffers a bit from the strong realism it signals, such as in the faithfully rendered B-25s in a hilly base (filmed in Mexico instead of Corsica) and the scenes in flight, etc. This collides with the openly absurd development of the plot.

The title of *Catch-22* refers to a clause in the Air Force rulebook. The rule wasn't actually there, but it could have been there, given the logic of the war, that is, the need to fight the enemy while at the same time acknowledging that killing is against the instinct of most soldiers. It says: if an airman wants to be grounded because of "combat fatigue," this can't be allowed — because by demonstrating that he doesn't like to fight, he's psychologically sound, and he can go on flying...! This is *Catch-22*.

The novel also has a rather colorful gallery of characters, including Milo Minderbinder, Major Major, Colonel Cathcart, General Dreedle, and Doc Daneeka.

The story ends with Yossarian about to row to Sweden. As a Swede, I think this is rather quaint.

17. J. G. Ballard

James Graham Ballard (1930-2009) never finished the training phase of his RAF days, but nonetheless, he makes it into this chapter. In his avant-garde fiction, he has a keen, symbolic eye for aircraft and for flying.

Ballard joined the RAF in 1954. After some basic training in England, he was sent to Canada for flight training, flying the North-American Harvard (aka. Texan). He aimed towards stationing in Bomber Command, and wished to fly the nuclear bomber Vulcan "with pieces of the sun in the bomb-bay" as he says in *The Kindness of Women*. This slightly embellished memoir was published in 1991.

After a while, Ballard realized that the Air Force wasn't the place for him. However, he had reached the solo-flying phase by then and knew enough about flying to have it feature in stories such as *The Unlimited Dream Company* (where the main character descends from the sky in a sports plane like an aluminum angel), *My Dream of Flying to Wake Island, Low-Flying Aircraft*, and again, *The Kindness of Women*. In the last book, the detection of a Hurricane wreck in an English river bed becomes a symbolic event of burying WWII, which always haunted Ballard.

Ballard was born in Shanghai, China, in 1930 as the son of an English factory manager. His family lived in relative luxury in the international settlement. In 1937 the Japanese attacked China but also let the international settlement remain. However, the countryside was still ravaged by war, and the young Ballard roamed it using the experience as a source of inspiration. Then, in 1941, the Japanese attacked the international settlement, and the British, French, and Americans became prisoners of war. This is referenced in Ballard's 1984 novel *Empire of the Sun*. The prison camp is located next to a Japanese airfield and planes, and the aerial warfare is a potent symbol of the whole drama.

18. Åke Hodell

A diverse range of characters has been featured in this exposé of aviators. Now only *the clown* remains: Åke Hodell. Not that being an air force pilot is a joke, but the Swede Hodell later became a pacifist and wrote absurdist lyrics. Hodell wrote a novel called *Skratta pajazzo* (*Laugh Clown*).

Åke Hodell (1919-2000) was born in Stockholm, and he was an early fan of flying. For instance, in 1928, the aviator pioneer Captain Albin Ahrenberg came to town in his Junkers F-13, a one-engine, enclosed cabin machine he used for public flights. It was pay-to-fly, which let the public participate in the exotic world of aviation. It was a hydroplane located in Dalarö in the Stockholm archipelago. When he was allowed into the plane and airborne, young Hodell constantly laughed. This was an example of flying as a drug, a strong fix.

During the preparation for WWII, Hodell joined the Swedish air force. His training took place at the Air War academy at Ljungbyhed in Scania. However, during a flight in July 1941, Hodell lost control of his J 9 Republic fighter and crashed. He was hospitalized and made a full recovery. After that, however, his flying days were over.

He became a pacifist and absurdist. We have nothing to say of this side of Hodell now, which, undoubtedly, was his main feature as a writer. Unfortunately, none of his work has been translated into English. However, the semi-biographical *Skratta pajazzo* was rather elegant: like Ballard in *The Kindness of Women*, he took his short life as an aviator and viably mythologized it.

Before he became a poet, in the 50s, Hodell met Sweden's most famous poet, Gunnar Ekelöf. They were quite similar ("anti-poets," anti-tradition), but Hodell was a bit nervous before the meeting and read up on diverse poetic subjects so that he was prepared for a relevant conversation. However, when they actually met, they started talking about engines. For his part, Ekelöf had once owned a Bugatti, and Hodell knew about aircraft engines. Only afterward, Hodell realized that they had actually been talking about poetry.

X. RIGORISM IN THE EAST I: THE SHOGUNS

In this chapter, we will look at rigorism and its historical appearance in Japan. Specifically, *the Shoguns*.[55] Like any Japanese ruler, the Shoguns occupied the role of *hegemon* under the Emperor. The Emperor was the chief of state; the Shogun was the executive ruler. The Emperor, the Mikado, was always there, from the beginning, as a holy institution, akin to the Pope of Rome. The Emperor was a symbolic figurehead of profoundly religious significance.

In the beginning, the Emperor ruled Japan directly. But in the 900s CE, the House of Fujiwara were hegemonic rulers. The title of the executive was *kampaku* (regent). These Fujiwaras were reputed to run a humane government, as courtiers, not warriors. They ruled with oratory and ceremony, not the sword. The harshest punishment was banishment. Marrying into the Imperial family was another power base for the Fujiwaras. One of the prominent men of this line was Michinaga Fujiwara, whose rule lasted for about 30 years at the turn of the 10th and 11th centuries. *The Tale of Genji* describes this political culture.

This kind of rule might sound okay. The following samurai-style was harder. But — wasn't the Fujiwara style also a bit irresponsible,

---

[55]   The sources of this chapter are Kinoshita, Storry, and Steensgaard. Japanese names are customarily given with the family name first. However, to have stringency in the index I've decided not to follow this custom. Instead, the names of Japanese historical persons are given in European fashion, with the family name last.

a bit weak? "To rule softly" is a contradiction of terms. The world wasn't ready for this finesse in early medieval times.

Fujiwara ruled, but the samurais were waiting in the wing. They were the warrior class, embodied by the clans Taira and Minamoto. They increased their power in different ways — military might was needed to keep order in the country, making sure the taxes were paid, and so on — but these two clans eventually started to feud among themselves. Taira won the first round of this battle and its head, Kiyomori Taira, gained a higher position at the court. He started practicing the old marriage policy à la Fujiwara. In 1171, for example, he had his daughter marry the eight-year-old Emperor.

Kiyomori has gone down in history as a villain, possibly because Minamoto later defeated the Taira, and the victor always writes the history. However, Kiyomori could be seen as a representative of the "copper age" people of Ovid: a man of a tougher mindset, yet not a barbarian, and the previous Fujiwara rule, can be seen as the silver age. Villain or not, there's a memorable 19th-century color print of Kiyomori where he stands on the patio of his villa and looks out over a snowy landscape, with the snow on the tree branches discreetly forming into skulls.

Kiyomori and his samurai took power; they lived by the sword and ruled with the sword. For example, the death penalty was re-instated in contrast to Fujiwara's time when *banishment* was the most torturous punishment. However, these refined Kyoto rulers now lost power and it was partly their own fault. At the end of the Fujiwara rule, different court parties had taken Tairas and Minamotos into their service, hardly suspecting that Fujiwara themselves would be totally outmaneuvered in the process. That said, these courtly rulers also left behind a heritage of *passion for culture* so that when the samurai became rulers, they also became interested in art. Toughness accompanied by cultural refinement became a samurai trait.

Taira had taken power and defeated Minamoto, but Minamoto soon rebelled and won. Its designated leader, Yoritomo Minamoto

Seii Tai-Shogun, had already established an office meaning "barbarian-beating commander." The title now became hereditary, and the Shogun became the dictator of the land, a kind of ruler *de facto* while the Emperor remained ruler *de jure.* The Shoguns had the role of hegemons, as mentioned previously. The name of this military government was *Bakufu,* "tent government" or "government behind the veil." The city of residence was Kamakura by the eastern seaboard. Moving away from Kyoto was necessary to start with a clean slate.

The Shogunate turned out as it did due to the previous government regime being corrupt and unstable. For example, Kiyomori Taira was still occupied with marriage policies and court intrigue. On the other hand, the Minamoto Bakufu came from a more independent power agency with greater continuity, providing some credibility. This meant a political maturation for Japan.

*****

Yoritomo died in the early 1190s following a fall from a horse. After Yoritomo's two young sons died, his wife Masako and her family Hojo took over as rulers, entitled *Shikken.* According to established tradition, only Minamotos could be Shoguns. But the Hojo reigned for a while with a steady hand, defending Japan against the Mongol invasions. However, they were beset by a rebellion, which was an attempt by the Emperor to rule directly.

This anti-Hojo rebellion was the *Kemmu Restauration* of the 1330s. The institute of the Emperor still held a lot of prestige even though the office-holder *per se* was relatively powerless. The story is reminiscent of contemporary European struggles around the Holy See: parties for and against the Pope were formed, but the institution was never questioned.

The Emperor was restored to full power. The Mikado had a legendary warrior to defend his cause, Masashige Kusunoki. At the final battle, when everything was lost, Masashige still fought on to the death, having reportedly said, "I wish I had seven lives to give for the fatherland": *Shisi sei hokoku*. During WWII, this was a motto for kamikaze pilots. All told, this is very legendary and very inspiring. It illustrates *in nuce* the role of willpower in history.

*****

In mere political terms, the Kemmu restoration failed. Instead, a new dynasty of Shoguns was established by Takauji Ashikaga. He didn't direct his campaigns against the Emperor himself (which would have been blasphemy) but against one of his advisers, Yoshisada Nitta. Takauji recruited many samurai to his cause, aiming to lead Japan in a Bakufu-style government, content with having the Emperor playing second fiddle.

Takauji won the civil war and reinstated the Shogunate. However, he moved the seat of government from Kamakura to Kyoto, which was a sign of weakness. This nullified the *leverage* the Kamakura seat implied. At Kyoto, the Bakufu was fair game for court intrigue, haggling, luxury, and pleasure. This Muromachi period saw the Bakufu decline, but it was also an era of cultural and economic blooming. For example, Japan now traded with China.

At the end of the 1400s, the last Ashikaga Shogun was dethroned by a warlord. After many battles, a new Shogun dynasty was established, the Tokugawa. However, essentially, the executive government of the shogun aside, things remained the same. The Emperor still officially ruled, and everyone was loyal to him, even the most ambitious *Daimyo* (samurai lord).

It was in 1603 that Ieyasu Tokugawa became hereditary Shogun. This required Minamoto lineage, and this, after some casuistry, he seemed to have. In the 1630s, the successor Iemitsu consolidated the country, and everything developed well, though some would say it did so in the fashion of a dictatorship. The Shogun owned 1/3 of Japanese land, allowing him to control the Emperor's livelihood, etc. Traditionally, the Shogun visited the Emperor in a reverent fashion, but eventually, this ceased. After Iemitsu, no Shogun visited his *Tenno* for two hundred years. The Shogun had absolute power, and the Emperor was isolated in his Kyoto palace. For example, he wasn't allowed to visit Daimyo. The hegemons ruled, and the Emperor was powerless — for the moment.

Iemitsu and his successors were able to close the country to the outside world, to prevent Japan from becoming a colony, protecting it from the approach of Westerners. Initially, this was a wise policy, but in the last half of the 19th century, the economy had stagnated, and Bakufu realized that the country had to be opened. Indeed, after the United States' protests, the insulation policy was ended in the 1850s, but the presence of strangers was very unpopular; they lived under ex-territorial rights, punishable only by their own governments, leaving Japan in a semi-colonial state.

Japan had surrendered, but the opposition to foreign intrusion was strong, especially in the anti-Bakufu circles of the imperial court. As a result, the Shogunate alone took on responsibility for the new policy; this was probably a surrender to the West, but what was the alternative? Bakufu made uncomfortable but sorely needed decisions: opening the country to obtain modern know-how, eventually enabling Japan to be brought in parity with the Western world. Indeed, the imperial party slogan of "kick out the barbarians and restore the Emperor" eventually became "restored imperial power and continued contact with the barbarians." Chauvinists could then expand the issue to "kick out the barbarians from all of Southeast Asia," which became the policy of action from 1905 onwards. Objectively speaking, this became a successful policy. Unfortunately, however, the colonial realms did fall for the Rising Sun onslaught, even though the final result didn't turn out as Japan expected.

The restoration of imperial rule quietly began in the early 19th century. An Emperor would make a trip outside of Kyoto, something that hadn't happened for a long time, to visit a specific villa in Shugaku built by a predecessor. The purpose for this may have been innocent, but people along the road who saw the imperial company cheered in a way that they never did for the shogun. For the rest of the 19th century, the Emperor and the court became the focus for groupings that were opposed to the Bakufu.

A new Shogun, a Tokugawa called Yoshinobu, was inaugurated in 1866. In 1867 Emperor Komei died and was succeeded by his 15-year-old son Mutsuhito who came to rule for 45 years. He had an active disposition and was the right person at the right time to hold this position, ruling like a Japanese version of William I of Prussia. He was precisely the "executive" Emperor that Japan desired. In November 1867, the Shogun voluntarily transferred power to the Emperor. By then, the Daimyo clans of Satsuma and Mori had succeeded in enforcing the view that it would be appropriate for the Shogun to resign at the time of the new Emperor's inauguration. The ceremony was held at the Nijo-Kyoto Castle in Kyoto, in the Ohiroma room. Nijo-Jo had been built by Ieyasu Tokugawa, who, among other things, had received the title of Shogun from the Emperor there.

Shogun Yoshinobu resigned, but various battles ensued. At the end of January 1868, immediately after the proclamation of the restored imperial regime, the army of the ex-Shogun attacked Kyoto. Their motivation was to save the Emperor from the harmful influence of the "outer, western" Daimyo Mori and Satsuma. The is said to have happened at the instigation of Shogun hang-arounds. The Shogun didn't want to take up arms, but neither did he want to leave his seat of power without a struggle. He expected to be an interim ruler under Mutsuhito. But during a three-day battle in the cities of Toba and Fushimi, located between Osaka and Kyoto, the Shogun army was defeated. The so-called "western" Daimyos defeated at Sekigahara in 1600 took revenge. Like Sekigahara, the outcome at Toba and Fushimi was partly decided by betrayal because on the last day of the battle, some of the Tokugawa forces simply switched sides. The Shogun went to Edo, where he later surrendered. However, some followers resisted, such as those at Ueno Heights in eastern Tokyo, Aizu-Wakamatsu in northern Honshu, and

Hakodate, Hokkaido. The Emperor received the last Shogun in June 1902 as an appointed prince, which was a great honor.

In general, the Tokugawa Shogunate went down with all guns blazing. Regardless of it being a lost cause, they didn't yield without a fight. They didn't just fade away like the Ashikaga Shogunate. Moreover, the Tokugawa regime wasn't utterly stagnant at the end, as it had already begun the modernization of Japan. At the time, progressive ideas weren't just monopolized by the opposition.

All told, the Japanese Bakufu remains a potent symbol for the will to power in history.

XI. RIGORISM IN THE EAST II: KANIKANĪTI

This chapter examines India, and the central part concerns deliberations upon a passage in the epic of *Mahābhārata*. This isn't a stylistic deviation from the historical content of the preceding chapters because the form of rigorism in the *Mahābhārata* is symbolized by a man, not a mythical being. It also illustrates the very tangible Indian tradition of the *Arthaśāstra*, an ancient handbook of statecraft with a Machiavellian outlook. Its authorship is attributed to Kauṭilya (375-283 BCE).

The *Arthaśāstra* is renowned as a formidable text. And the passage that we will discuss here is a viable expression of the *Arthaśāstra's* ethos. It is not tyrannical but it doesn't shy away from ruling with an iron rod. The force of arms is always present in the background. The *Arthaśāstra* does not endorse faceless bureaucrats or weak irresponsible governance of the clerical kind. This form of rigorism proceeds from an element of Indian statecraft called *upāyas* (means). There were four *upāyas*: *sāntva* (sometimes called *sāman*), *dāna*, *bheda*, and *daṇḍa;* respectively, *conciliation, gift, sowing dissent,* and *force of arms*. As we see, the two former ones were positive sanctions. The two latter were negative, reminding us of a similar attitude expressed by Machiavelli, who also knows how to deploy "the stick or the carrot" approach.

The chapter of the *Mahābhārata* (Mbh) where we find the central text in question is called *Kaṇikanīti* (Kaṇika's Lesson). Some editions exclude this or refer to it in the appendix (as in the Poona edition). In Book One of Mbh, *Ādiparvan*, we are told how the offspring of the two branches of Clan Bhārata were raised together in the court of King Dhṛtarāṣṭra. His own sons, Kauravas, had to coexist with those of his dead brother, the Pāṇḍavas. King Dhṛtarāṣṭra placates the Pāṇḍavas by appointing the oldest as successor to the throne. In this story phase, the Pāṇḍavas are generally on an upsurge. They launch military conquests and are popular among the citizens, while the Kauravas feel left aside. Dhṛtarāṣṭra then wonders what to do about this, so that the Pāṇḍavas don't become too popular at the expense of his sons, the Kauravas. He consults the minister Kaṇika for guidance in the *Kaṇikanīti* passage, comprising some 200 lines.

The king asks: "Shall I have peace or war with the Pāṇḍavas?" The minister then answers him in "sharp words," *vacanam tīkṣṇam* (line 9). But, unfortunately, most of them are abstract, and only the last eight lines provide specific advice on dealing with the Pāṇḍavas. The recommendation is to protect himself against the Pāṇḍavas because they are stronger.

Kaṇika's lecture is informally divided into three parts. Part one and three bestow general advice. This is the epigrammatic rigorism of the East, the wisdom of a chess game applied to practical geopolitics. *The enemy's enemy is my friend, allies are merely friendly enemies* — which is also the gist of the *Arthaśāstra*. The second part of *Kaṇikanīti* begins with a question from the king that the minister answers with a fable, which illustrates rigorist statecraft well. The beginning and incentive for Indian fable literature was an introduction to statecraft for young princes. The original fables were not merely "fairy tales and animal stories," which we in the West tend to see them as. The ancient Indian fable was "Machiavellianism made popular, rigorism for the budding prince," so to speak. According to Keith,[56] fable collections such as the *Pañcatantra* were composed as political handbooks, not collections of folk tales. In lines 47-48, *Kaṇika* mentions the *upāyas*, the four means of dealing with an enemy. A king shall kill his enemy (*hanyād amitram*) by using any or all of them, *sāntva, dāna, bheda, and daṇḍa*:

---

[56] p. 246.

> *hanyād amitraṃ sāntvena tathā dānena vā punaḥ*
> *tathaiva bhedadaṇḍābhyaṃ sarvopāyaiḥ praśātayet*
> You shall crush the enemy by using *sāntva, dāna, bheda,* or
> *daṇḍa;* with all the *upāyas* he shall be annihilated.

Dhṛtarāṣṭra then asks how he should go about doing this, and then
Kaṇika tells his enlightening fable. You could say that it's a tale of
"fox-like cunning," with the fox here played by a jackal.

In a forest lived a jackal, a tiger, a mouse, a wolf, and a mungo.
Once, they saw a deer that they wanted to catch and devour.
However, since it was too fast and too intelligent — *javasampanno,
buddhiśālī*[57] — to be overpowered by the strongest of them, the
tiger, they had to sit down and deliberate. The jackal then proposed
that the mouse would consume its legs while it slept; then, the tiger
would attack it. "Then we can eat to our hearts' content," *tato vai
bhakṣayiṣyāmaḥ sarve muditamānasaḥ.*[58]

The plan is implemented, and it works, the deer is killed the way
the jackal planned it, and then he tells the others to go and perform
their religious ablutions while he guards the prey. While doing this,
he deliberates on what to do next, deep in thoughts — *cintāparamo
bhutvā.*[59]

Then his allies return, one by one — and he chases them off, one
by one. This is the pattern for the rest of the story. First, the tiger's
pride is hurt when the jackal fools him that the mouse had said it
was a shame that he helped the tiger to kill prey — in two minds
after hearing this, the tiger leaves, henceforth planning to kill wild
prey by only relying on his strength.

The mouse is chased away by the jackal cheating him, saying that
the mungo has said that deer meat isn't so tasty; he would love to kill
and eat the mouse. The mouse gets scared and runs away.

---

[57] Line 58.

[58] Linc 61.

[59] Line 67.

The jackal fools the wolf into believing that the tiger is mad at him, the tiger just now being on his way with his wife ... the wolf flees.

Then the mungo returns from his religious bath. The jackal tells him that he, the jackal, has vanquished the others by sheer physical force (*svabāhubalam āśritya*).[60] Finally, the jackal offers the mungo the deer meat if he's ready to fight for it — which he's not, so he voluntarily leaves. Thus the jackal could happily devour the deer meat on his own.

The idea is to be sly, use cunning. Use the pattern of the four upāyas. Use different means against different enemies. By referring to the tiger's pride (vaguely, this is *sāntva*); by sowing dissent between the mouse and the mungo (*bheda*); by scaring the wolf with the supposed anger of the tiger (*daṇḍa*); by intimating to the mungo that the jackal has scared the others away (also *daṇḍa*). Kaṇika's coda is this: "The shy shall be crushed by awakening their fear; the brave by being met with respect; the greedy by being offered gifts, and equals and inferiors by showing strength."[61] Again, this might be seen as general wisdom, not applicable to the situation of defeating the Pāṇḍavas — for, in the power struggle between the families, this group of five brothers is treated as a collective, not as five separate actors. This might illustrate the unnecessary nature of *Kaṇikanīti* from a mere dramatic point of view, making it inessential to the story at large — and hence its relegation to an appendix or excluded entirely. It's interesting, though, that Narayan, in his short, novel-length Mbh-version, does include the passage, which is where we first read the Kaṇika episode.

Kaṇikanīti is fierce in tone and content, much more so than most of the *Arthaśāstra*. For instance, in lines 104-105, Kaṇika says that if your relative — son, friend, brother, father, or teacher — becomes your enemy, you should kill him. On the same subject, the *Arthaśāstra* states that the enemy primarily should be placated with

---

[60] Relying on the strength of one's own arm, line 93.

[61] Lines 101-102.

the positive sanctions of conciliation and gifts (*sāntva* and *dāna*).[62] The fierce attitude continues in the rest of *Kaṇikanīti*, which advises the king to be ruthless toward his enemies — such as saying one thing and doing another, always being vigilant, trusting no one, etc.

✳✳✳✳✳

Finally, we shall provide some conceptual background by looking at scientific Indian literature from ancient times, which covers the *upāyas*. We will examine the *Arthaśāstra* and *Dharmaśāstra*, the latter in the form of *Manu's Laws* (*Manusmṛti* or *Mānava-dharmaśāstra*).

The *Arthaśāstra* was directed at practical advice and hands-on instruction, while *Dharmaśāstra* had a more elevated, moral character. That said, there is not much difference between the two. The *Arthaśāstra* isn't all "raw Machiavellianism," it's exceptionally sane and in harmony with everyday morality. *Manu's Laws*, to a certain extent, even seems to be based on the *Arthaśāstra*.[63]

As Sharma[64] points out, the *Arthaśāstra* is a treatise of political science in addition to being a deliberation on the science of welfare and riches, as the title denotes: *artha*, Skt. for *riches*. Trautmann[65] says that the *Arthaśāstra* is the earliest preserved work of its kind, one to which all the later *Arthaśāstras* are indebted. Also, it's more elaborate and detailed than any of its followers. It was completed around 150 CE.[66]

As for *Manu's Laws*, it's a *smṛti*, a holy text, being a regulation of life in the moral and religious vein. It is the oldest that India has, completed about the same time as the *Arthaśāstra*. As for the *Mahābhārata*, the source for the *Kaṇikanīti* text, it was completed

---

[62] Shamasastry, p. 435.

[63] Trautmann, p. 185.

[64] p. 22.

[65] p. 3.

[66] Ibid, p. 184.

slightly after this, around 400 CE;[67] thus, like the other documents of the study, belonging to the era of classical Indian antiquity.

Obviously, *Kaṇikanīti* is much shorter than the other two, a five-page episode in an epic, while the others are substantial handbooks. We should remember this when comparing their meaning. *Kaṇikanīti* tells the king to use the *upāyas* as offensive weapons to crush the enemy. As for the morality of his fable, even *sāntva* is used offensively and deviously. Conversely, the *Arthaśāstra* and *Manu's Laws* have a more variegated approach, such as stressing the positive nature of *sāntva* and *dāna,* and the negative approach of *bheda* and *daṇḍa.* One should commence by using *sāntva*; if that leads nowhere, then try *dāna*, then *bheda*, and, lastly, if everything else has failed, use *daṇḍa.*

Generally, the *Arthaśāstra* states that *sāntva* is the means for conciliation and peacemaking. The lesson seems that merely crushing an enemy creates new problems, which even the ancient Romans knew.

However, in the context where we met the fierce Kaṇika, the plot subsequently moves into the territories of *daṇḍa* and *bheda*. It's the underlying logic behind the transition of the world from the Sat Yuga to the Treta Yuga. A world crisis ensues, placing the two branches of the Bhārata clan in a devastating war with millions dying. The Pāṇḍavas win. Then a new era emerges to become the iron age of our times. This era of rigorism continued until 2012. From then onwards, major war seems impossible, as we've written previously in Chapter Two and *Actionism*.

War or no war — any responsible ruler must use either positive or negative sanctions. No ruler can solely govern with gifts and conciliation — *dāna* and *sāntva*. Politics is about priorities, about enforcing one's will on the world, and for this, a reasonable use of force (*daṇḍa*) is also required.

---

[67]   Dimcock, p. 125.

LITERATURE

Adcock, F. E. *Antikens krigskonst*. 1, Greker och makedonier. Stockholm: Prisma, 1966

Andolf, Göran. *Historien mellan 1815 och 1870*. Stockholm: Esselte stadium, 1976

Arrian. *The Campaigns of Alexander*. London: Penguin Books, 1971

Ballard, J. G. *Empire of the Sun. London*: Gollancz, 1984

Ballard, J. G. *The Kindness of Women*. London: HarperCollins, 1991

Beaufre, André. *Modern strategi för fred och krig (Introduction à la stratégie*, 1963). Stockholm: Prisma, 1966

Cooper, Duff. *Talleyrand*. Stockholm: Norstedts 1951

Bjöl, Erling: *En ny världsordning*. Höganäs: Bokorama, 1987

Bjöl, Erling and Hjortsö, *Leo*. Romarriket. Stockholm: Bonniers, 1983

Boberg, Stig. *1700-talets historia*. Stockholm: Esselte studium, 1973

Boberg, Stig. *Upplysningstiden*. Stockholm: Bonnier, 1985

Bullock, Alan. *Hitler – En studie i tyranni (A Study in Tyranny*, 1962). Stockholm: Prisma 1966

Bühler, G. (translator) *The Laws of Manu*. Delhi: Motilal Banarsidass, 1975

Caesar, Julius. *Kriget i Gallien (De bello gallico)*. Stockholm: Natur & Kultur, 1963

Calleman, Carl Johan. *The Mayan Calendar and the Transformation of Consciousness*. Rochester, Vermont: Bear & Company, 2004

Dahl, Roald. *Going Solo*. London: Jonathan Cape, 1986

Dimcock, Edward C. *The Literatures of India – an Introduction*. Chicago: The University of Chicago Press, 1974

Dumrath, O. H. *Det XIX:e århundradet*. Stockholm: Geber, 1899

Estlander, B. *Allmänna historien i berättelser*. Stockholm: P. A. Norstedt & söners förlag, 1924

Fuller, J. F. C. *Julius Caesar: Man, Soldier and Tyrant*. London: Eyre & Spottiswoode, 1965

Furuhagen, Hans. *Grekernas värld*. Stockholm: Bonniers, 1982

Herodotus. *The Histories*. London: Penguin Books, 1972

Hodell, Åke. *Skratta pajazzo*. Stockholm: Författarförlaget, 1983

Johansson, Alf W. *Europas krig*. Stockholm: Tiden, 1989

Josephsson, Ragnar. Karl XII som estet *in* Jonasson, Gustaf (ed.). *Historia kring Karl XII*. Stockholm: Wahlström & Widstrand, 1964

Jünger, Ernst. *Das abenteuerliche Herz. Figuren und Capriccios*. Hamburg: Hanseatische Verlagsanstalt, 1938

Jünger, Ernst. *Eumeswil*. Stuttgart: Klett-Cotta, 1977

Keith, A. Berridale. *A History of Sanskrit Literature*. Oxford: Clarendon Press, 1928

Kerényi, Karl. *Grekiska gudar och myter*. Stockholm: Natur & Kultur, 1955

Kiley, Frederick and McDonald, Walter (editors). *A 'Catch-22' Casebook*. New York: Crowell, 1973

Kinoshita, June and Palevsky, Nicholas. *Gateway to Japan*. Tokyo: Kodansha, 1990

Kluge, Alexander. Slaget (*Schlachtbeschreibung*, 1964). Stockholm: Norstedts, 1964

Liddell Hart, Sir Basil Henry. *På andra sidan kullen* (The Other Side of the Hill, 1965). Stockholm: Natur & Kultur, 1988

Livy. *Rome and the Mediterranean*. London: Penguin Books, 1976

Machiavelli, Niccolò. *The Prince* (*Il principe*, 1532). London: Penguin Books, 1977

Moltke, Helmuth von. Lefnadssaga, bref, tal m.m. *Sine loco et anno*

Montgomery of Alamein. *Krigskonstens historia* (*A History of Warfare*, 1968). Lund: Militärlitteraturföreningen, 1970

Narayan, R. K. *The Mahābhārata*. London: Heinemann, 1978

Plutarch. *The Age of Alexander*. London: Penguin Books, 1988

Plutarch. *The Fall of the Roman Republic*. London: Penguin Books, 1984

Plutarch. *The Rise and Fall of Athens*. London: Penguin Books, 1960

P:son Nilsson, Martin. *Olympen*. Stockholm: Gebers, 1922

Roy, Pratap Chandra (translator). *Ādiparvan*. Calcutta: Bhārata Press, 1883

Serrano, Miguel. *Adolf Hitler, the Ultimate Avatar*. (*Adolf Hitler – el último avatāra*, 1984). Australia: Hermitage Helm Corpus, 2014

Serrano, Miguel. *The Golden Thread. (El cordón dorado*, 1978) London: Wermod & Wermod, 2017

Shamasastry, R. (translator) *Kauṭilya's Arthaśāstra.* Mysore: Government Oriental Library Series, 1915

Sharma, Ram Sharan. *Aspects of Political Ideas and Institutions in Ancient India.* Delhi: Motilal Banarsidass, 1991

Spengler, Oswald. *Människan och tekniken (Man and Technics,* 1931). Stockholm: Hugo Gebers förlag, 1931

Spengler, Oswald. *Västerlandets undergång (The Decline of the West,* 1922). Stockholm: Atlantis, 1997

Steensgaard, Niels. *Upptäckternas tid.* Höganäs: Bra Böcker, 1985

Storry, Richard. *Det moderna Japans historia (A History of Modern Japan).* Stockholm: Prisma, 1969

Suetonius. *Kejsarbiografier.* Stockholm: Wahlström & Widstrand, 2001

Sukthankar, Vishnu S. (editor) *Ādiparvan (Mahābhārata,* vol. 1). Poona: Bhandarkar Oriental Research Institute, 1933

Tacitus. *Annaler I-VI.* Stockholm: Forum, 1966

Tacitus. *Annaler XI-XVI.* Stockholm: Forum, 1968

Tingsten, Herbert. *Sällskap för mina tankar.* Stockholm: Norstedts, 1971

Trautmann, Thomas R. *Kautīlya and the Arthaśāstra.* Leiden: E. J. Brill, 1971

Voltaire. Karl XII *(Histoire de Charles XII,* Roi de Suède, 1731). Stockholm: Klassikerförlaget, 1993

Webster, Paul. *Antoine de Saint-Exupéry: the Life and Death of the Little Prince.* London: Macmillan, 1993

Weibull, Curt. *Historiska problem och utvecklingslinjer*. Stockholm: Aldus / Bonniers, 1962

Wilcock, David. *The Synchronicity Key*. New York: Dutton, 2013

Wretman, Enrique and Olofsson, Sven Ingemar. *Spaniens historia*. Stockholm: Natur & Kultur, 1969

Yorck von Wartenburg, *Ludwig. Napoleon as A General*. London: Kegan, Paul, Trench, Trubner & Co, 1902

INDEX

ABOUT THE AUTHOR

Lennart Svensson (1965-) is primarily known for his philosophy of life, *Actionism* (2017). He has published several works, in English and Swedish, including novels and essays. His other prominent non-fiction books are *Ernst Jünger — A Portrait* (2014), *Science Fiction Seen from the Right* (2016), and *Commanders* (2018).

9 780645 212648